Psychic Protection

The Spiritual Self-Defense Guide to Angelic Protection, Karma, Soul Cleansing, Aura Healing, and Defending Against Negative Energy

© Copyright 2023 - All rights reserved.

The content contained within this book may not be reproduced, duplicated, or transmitted without direct written permission from the author or the publisher.

Under no circumstances will any blame or legal responsibility be held against the publisher, or author, for any damages, reparation, or monetary loss due to the information contained within this book, either directly or indirectly.

Legal Notice:

This book is copyright protected. It is only for personal use. You cannot amend, distribute, sell, use, quote or paraphrase any part of or the content within this book, without the consent of the author or publisher.

Disclaimer Notice:

Please note the information contained within this document is for educational and entertainment purposes only. All effort has been executed to present accurate, up-to-date, reliable, and complete information. No warranties of any kind are declared or implied. Readers acknowledge that the author is not engaging in the rendering of legal, financial, medical, or professional advice. The content within this book has been derived from various sources. Please consult a licensed professional before attempting any techniques outlined in this book.

By reading this document, the reader agrees that under no circumstances is the author responsible for any losses, direct or indirect, that are incurred as a result of the use of the information contained within this document, including, but not limited to, errors, omissions, or inaccuracies.

Your Free Gift
(only available for a limited time)

Thanks for getting this book! If you want to learn more about various spirituality topics, then join Mari Silva's community and get a free guided meditation MP3 for awakening your third eye. This guided meditation mp3 is designed to open and strengthen ones third eye so you can experience a higher state of consciousness. Simply visit the link below the image to get started.

https://spiritualityspot.com/meditation

Table of Contents

INTRODUCTION 1
CHAPTER 1: WHY DO WE NEED PSYCHIC PROTECTION? 3
CHAPTER 2: PREPARE YOUR PSYCHE FIRST..................................13
CHAPTER 3: SOUL AND KARMA CLEANSING 23
CHAPTER 4: CLEANSING YOUR SPACE AND OTHERS 32
CHAPTER 5: POST-CLEANSE: HEALING YOUR AURA 45
CHAPTER 6: CALLING UPON ANGELS FOR PROTECTION 55
CHAPTER 7: STONES, PLANTS, AND SYMBOLS OF PROTECTION 64
CHAPTER 8: BREAKING CURSES, HEXES, AND ATTACHMENTS 73
CHAPTER 9: SHIELDING YOURSELF AND YOUR LOVED ONES............84
CHAPTER 10: WARDING RITUALS TO PROTECT YOUR HOME...............96
CONCLUSION..109
HERE'S ANOTHER BOOK BY MARI SILVA THAT YOU MIGHT LIKE 111
YOUR FREE GIFT (ONLY AVAILABLE FOR A LIMITED TIME) 112
REFERENCES..113

Introduction

People communicate with each other's energies all the time. Setting boundaries for energetic communication can be challenging. However, protecting yourself from other people's energies is critical to maintaining your energetic balance and a healthy mental state. Some people are more sensitive to others' vibes and have difficulty separating themselves from the energetic influences affecting them. They can pick up people's emotions more easily, which affects them. However, even if you do not belong to this category, stress, fatigue, and the lack of boundaries can make you more vulnerable to negative influences and psychic attacks. Either way, it doesn't hurt to consciously protect yourself from energetic effects.

Psychic connections can be beneficial. For example, they can help you bond in relationships or help you better understand how you relate to others and yourself as a person. However, it is unhealthy to allow people who aren't close to you or wish you harm to impact your vibes. Even if their emotions and vibes are positive, sometimes, you merely want to be aware of your feelings. Being self-aware is critical to understanding why you have specific sentiments. You cannot achieve this if you're always affected by other people's energies. Let's say you're in a good place emotionally but spend time with a friend going through a rough time. You'll feel the effects of their negative vibes and may have trouble separating your emotions from theirs.

Psychic protection can help you separate other people's feelings and thoughts from yours. For those more sensitive (temporarily or permanently) to others' energies, picking up their feelings is as easy as catching a cold. Learning to barricade your feelings will help you identify other people's vibes, filter these feelings, or block them if needed.

This book introduces you to setting psychic boundaries and creating a safe space for your emotions. Through practical exercises, you'll better understand who you are and how others' energies affect you. They will help you center and ground yourself to ward off and release unwanted influences. Paying attention to your chakras and auras is crucial to containing your energy and establishing psychic boundaries.

After emphasizing the importance of psychic protection, this book teaches you how to prepare your psyche by providing tips and exercises to raise your vibration and sharpen your psychic skills. You'll be provided plenty of techniques, cleansing rituals, and instructions for thoroughly cleansing your soul. Moreover, the book includes several simple cleansing rituals and methods for clearing your space and those around you. Once cleaned, you must heal your aura and reverse previous damage.

Several chapters are dedicated to different tools you can use for psychic protection. First, you learn to summon your guardian angels or an archangel to ask for their protection from psychic attacks. Then, you'll master the art of using protective crystals, plants, and symbols for protection. Also, you are taught how to use spells to defend against curses, hexes, and unwanted links, attachments, or relationships. Lastly, this book offers plenty of user-friendly ways to protect yourself at home or work, ward off negative vibes from your home, and protect your loved ones, pets, or children - whether they're near you or far away.

Chapter 1: Why Do We Need Psychic Protection?

Encounters with other people can lead to energy contamination.
https://unsplash.com/photos/W3Jl3jREpDY?utm_source=unsplash&utm_medium=referral&utm_content=creditShareLink

When starting on the spiritual self-defense journey, many people ask why psychic protection is necessary. This question most often arises when performing rituals, including the manifestation of energy, emphasizing protection even when the ritual is for love, money, or healing. Mundane people wonder why this protection is needed, what dangers exist, and whether psychic attacks are so dangerous they require proper protection. However, there are no simple answers to these questions. You must first grasp the concept of energy and how it affects you to understand why you need protection from the unseen.

Consider this. During the day, you engage with multiple people, whether at home, grocery shopping, or just walking down the street. Each person has an energy aura, which directly affects their energy field. When you engage with these people, you're bound to be affected by their emotional state and energy. Your interactions with others create emotional connections, a natural aspect of being human, and whether you're aware of it or not, these emotional connections negatively affect you. Of course, this isn't to say all interactions can negatively affect your energy, but only those with harmful projections.

According to the laws of physics, everything in the world is made up of energy in motion, including your existence. So, in this context, your daily encounters with other people, whether family, friends, colleagues, or random strangers, are essentially the meeting of energetic bodies. This encounter leads to energy contamination. Indeed, you cannot see this energy, just as you can't see germs with your naked eye, but it doesn't make the fact that germs exist any less accurate. Energy permeates everything around you.

For instance, emotions are energy. Have you ever walked into a room where two people have just finished a heated argument, and you felt the tension and heavy atmosphere without being aware of the situation? This feeling of discomfort and agitation is normal. Even if you don't possess psychic abilities, your body will still react to invisible stimuli. They can influence your mood, stress levels, and overall well-being.

Another example of how energy affects your thoughts and emotions is when you meet someone for the first time and feel instantly drawn to them, or conversely, feel discomfort or unease. What do you think this initial impression is? Or, as youngsters say, what do you think a person's vibes are? They're the energetic connection between you and the other person. Similarly, if you've had a gut feeling about something and later found out your intuition was right, this intuitive response results from energy sensing it, even if you cannot see it.

Energy comes in many forms (discussed later in the chapter), but you must be especially careful when dealing with negative energy. Negative energies and psychic attacks are energy harmfully affecting you. Negative energy can be derived from many sources, including the environment, objects, or people with negative emotions or intentions. If you're exposed to this energy for long periods, it can be mentally and physically draining. On the other hand, psychic attacks are intentional and always direct energy attacks from one person to another. Although the intention behind these attacks can range from mild annoyance to fully-fledged hatred, they manifest in various ways, like nightmares, sudden illness, mental drain, or inexplicable dread or anxiety.

The need for psychic protection doesn't always stem from apparent danger, but it remains crucial, nonetheless. Many people misunderstand the need for psychic protection only when there's an evil spirit to ward off or a need to defend themselves against known attacks from their detractors. However, potential threats can take on many forms, and it's always best to be prepared for them. Psychic attacks are much like curses, except they don't require ritual magic tools. However, the impact is pretty much the same, i.e., devastating. People who practice psychic attacks don't need to rely on candles, symbols, altars, or rituals but instead manifest their negative energy and intuition to bring harm, suffering, or misfortune to their victim.

Therefore, psychic protection should be an absolute essential, especially for those involved in energy work or spiritual magic. Everything is made up of energy, meaning your energy fields interact with those around you continuously, making you vulnerable to negative energies and psychic attacks. These can severely affect your physical, emotional, and mental well-being. Psychic protection will come in handy; it acts as your shield against these negative forces and allows you to maintain a positive state of mind. Regular protection techniques like grounding, visualization, and cleansing strengthen your energetic boundaries and increase your resilience to negative energies, allowing you to navigate life with greater ease and positivity.

Understanding Energy

In the context of psychic protection and energy work, energy refers to the life force that permeates everything in the universe, tangible and intangible. It is the invisible force flowing within and around you, shaping your experiences and interactions with the world. This energy is neither good nor bad; it simply is. It can be positive or negative, depending on how it is harnessed and utilized. In energy work, practitioners aim to tap into this force and manipulate it to achieve specific outcomes, such as healing, manifestation, or psychic protection. Understanding the nature of energy and how it interacts with your energetic fields is crucial if you plan to engage in energy work or psychic protection. There are different energies, including:

1. **Personal Energy:** The energy generated and emitted from your body. It is influenced by your thoughts, emotions, and physical state and can be felt by others in your immediate vicinity.
2. **Environmental Energy:** This refers to energy in the physical environment around you. It can be influenced by factors such as the weather, geographical location, and human activity.
3. **Universal Energy:** The energy that exists throughout the universe and is often associated with spiritual or metaphysical beliefs. It is the source of all life and the driving force behind many natural phenomena.
4. **Vibrational Energy:** The frequency or vibration of energy, positive or negative. Higher vibrational energies, such as love and joy, benefit your well-being, while lower vibrational energies, such as fear and anger, negatively impact your mental, emotional, and physical health.
5. **Elemental Energy:** The energy associated with earth, air, fire, and water elements. It is often used in rituals and spells and has specific properties and associations that can be harnessed for different purposes.

Energy-Work Exercises

Do some energy work exercises to better understand and feel the energy surrounding you. Energy manipulation is defined as the practice of directing and manipulating the energy flow within and around you. This energy should be considered a force that permeates all things and can be accessed and used through many techniques and practices. Different energies can be manipulated, including spiritual, emotional, and physical.

Spiritual energy is the energy present in the universe and connects all things. Emotional energy is the energy we generate through emotions and feelings. Physical energy is the energy that powers your body and keeps you alive.

Energy manipulation uses various techniques to increase, direct, or remove energy. Some of these techniques include visualization, meditation, breathwork, and movement. By practicing energy manipulation, individuals can learn to balance and enhance their energy levels, clear blockages, and promote healing. Energy manipulation can be used for manifestation, and manifestation techniques are based on the idea that everything is made up of energy, including thoughts and emotions. By focusing your thoughts and intentions, you can direct the energy flow toward a specific goal or outcome, including manifesting abundance, success, love, and happiness.

Below are some techniques to manifest and manipulate energy:

- **Creating an Energy Ball**

    To create a ball of energy, follow these steps:
    1. Sit or stand comfortably in a quiet, relaxed environment. Close your eyes and take a few deep breaths to center yourself.
    2. Visualize a ball of light in the center of your body, just below your navel. This ball can be any color, but many visualize it as white or gold.
    3. As you inhale, imagine you are drawing energy up from the earth and into your body, filling the ball with energy. As you exhale, imagine the ball expanding and growing brighter.
    4. Continue to breathe and visualize the energy ball growing larger and brighter. You might feel a tingling or warmth in your hands.
    5. Once the ball of energy is large enough, you can direct it to a specific area or use it for healing, protection, or manifestation.

- **Energy Sensing Exercise**

    The energy-sensing exercise is designed to help you become more aware of the energy around and within you. To do this exercise, follow these steps:
    1. Find a space where you can sit comfortably and without interruption. This space can be indoors or outdoors, but ensure you have privacy and won't be disturbed.

2. Close your eyes and take a few deep breaths to relax your body and quiet your mind. If you have tension in your body, consciously release it as you exhale.
3. Once you are relaxed, bring your attention to the sensations in your body. Notice any physical sensations, such as tingling, warmth, or pressure. Don't judge or analyze the sensations. Simply observe them.
4. Gradually expand your awareness to include the space around your body. Notice any changes in the sensations. You may feel a shift in energy or a sense of expansion.
5. With your expanded awareness, tune into the energy around you. You could feel a subtle vibration or hum or sense a particular quality or color of energy. Pay attention to the impressions you receive.
6. Scan your body from head to toe, noticing the areas where you feel a change in energy. You may feel areas of tension or blockage or openness and flow.
7. Bring your attention back to your breath and take a few more deep breaths. Notice how you feel after this exercise. You should feel more grounded, centered, and connected to the energy around you.

Remember, this exercise is not about achieving a specific outcome; it's about cultivating your energy awareness and ability to sense it. With practice, you will sense energy more easily and accurately.

- **Energy Projection**

Energy projection intentionally sends energy from your body to a specific target or area. This projection can be used for various purposes, such as healing, protection, or manifestation. Here's a step-by-step guide for an energy projection exercise:

1. Find a quiet and comfortable space where you won't be disturbed. Sit or stand comfortably with your feet firmly on the ground.
2. Close your eyes and take a few deep breaths, allowing yourself to relax and let go of the tension or stress in

your body.
3. Visualize a ball of bright, white light in the center of your body, just below your belly button. This ball of light represents your energy and power.
4. Focus your attention on the body area where you feel the most energy or sensation. It could be your hands, your chest, or your forehead.
5. Consciously direct your energy to that area by imagining the ball of light expanding and filling that space.
6. Once you feel a strong connection to that area, imagine directing the energy outward toward your intended target, a person, a place, or an object.
7. Visualize a beam of light extending from your body to the target, carrying your energy.
8. Keep focusing on the target and visualize your energy being received and absorbed by the target.
9. When you feel ready, slowly bring your awareness back to your body and the ball of light in your center.
10. Take a few deep breaths, and when you're ready, slowly open your eyes.

Remember, always use energy projection with positive intentions and respect for others. Also, grounding yourself afterward to release excess energy and return to a state of balance is important.

- **Energy Shielding**

Energy shielding is a technique using your energy to create a protective shield around yourself. This shield can help you to ward off negative energy or influences from others and promote a sense of safety and security. Here's a step-by-step guide for an energy shielding exercise:

1. Find a quiet and comfortable space where you won't be disturbed. Sit or stand comfortably with your feet firmly on the ground.
2. Close your eyes and take a few deep breaths, allowing yourself to relax and let go of the tension or stress in your body.

3. Visualize a ball of bright, white light in the center of your body, just below your belly button. This ball of light represents your energy and power.
4. Imagine this ball of light expanding and surrounding your body like a protective bubble. See it getting larger and stronger with each breath you take.
5. Set an intention for your energy shield. You can use a simple statement or affirmation, such as *"I am protected and safe from negative energy or influences."*
6. As you continue to visualize your energy shield, focus on the safety and protection it provides. You may feel warmth, peace, or calmness.
7. If you sense negative energy or unwanted influences trying to enter your energy shield, simply visualize them bouncing off and returning to the universe.
8. When you're ready to end the shielding practice, slowly bring your awareness back to your body and the ball of light in your center.
9. Take a few deep breaths, and when you're ready, slowly open your eyes.

You can experiment with different colors, shapes, and sizes for your energy shield or program it with a specific intention or purpose.

Why You Need Psychic Protection

There's no shortage of negativity in this world and numerous ways for this negative energy to reach you. Therefore, psychic protection is essential to maintain a healthy and balanced energy field. Whether the negative energies affecting you are intentional or unintentional, they can have a detrimental effect on your overall well-being. Psychic protection is particularly important for people sensitive to energy, like empaths or psychics, because they are more susceptible to absorbing the negative energies from their environment. Here's why it's essential to have psychic protection for yourself and your family:

1. Physical Harm

Properly utilizing techniques to manifest protection energy can help safeguard you against physical harm and other threats posed by psychic attacks. However, this doesn't mean psychic protection can deflect physical attacks. Instead, it's a more subtle manner of guiding you out of harm's way. Protection magic equips you with intuitive guidance to protect you from potential threats. When you utilize psychic protection, you may not even realize when you're saved from dangerous situations.

2. Harmful Energy

Harmful energy is derived from the unconscious remnants of day-to-day living, for instance, sadness, arguments, anger, or illness. This energy can cause physical, emotional, and mental discomfort, but most people don't notice because they're used to feeling this way. When using psychic protection, you'll stay protected from this harmful energy that drains your energy and dulls your mood.

3. Harmful Judgments

Thoughts are powerful forms of energy manifesting real consequences, even if they're not physically present. When you judge or project negative thoughts onto another person, you could harm them psychically and vice versa. While judging or comparing people is natural, the intention behind your thoughts is important. When people condemn or even name-call or hate someone, they are psychically attacking them. So, you should be mindful of your words and thoughts toward others. The same goes for other people, but since you can't control their thoughts, practicing psychic protection techniques is best to protect yourself from their harmful judgment (discussed in detail in the following chapters).

4. Psychic Vampires

You've probably encountered the term "psychic vampire" at least once. This term refers to someone who drains other people's energy without realizing what they're doing. These people are not self-aware or consider the negative effect they have on others. Psychic vampires often have mental, emotional, or physical issues, so they seek out those who burn brightly and feed on their energies. However, this behavior only brings them down further, and ultimately, they become shunned by others. Using techniques to protect you psychically can help protect you from being drained by psychic vampires.

5. Mesmerism

Mesmerism is a psychic attack suppressing an individual's will, caused by charming and convincing them with hypnotic effects. It is a mind control similar to brainwashing and is often unintentional or seen as harmless by the mesmerist. However, when an individual's discernment and intuition are suspended, it can be damaging. Some metaphysicians explain that the mesmerist projects vital life force, such as prana or akasha, from their eyes to charm, seduce, and control the target. The mesmerism's energy is soft and seductive to enrapture the victim. Psychic protection comes in handy when dealing with mesmeric individuals.

6. Past Life Energies

Some believe that negative energies can attach to the soul and follow from one life to the next until an underlying issue is confronted and resolved. These energies can be present from birth or activated when a similar situation in the current life is encountered. Where a person was cursed in a past life, that curse or its residual patterns are carried into their present existence. It can be challenging to differentiate between the effects of your karma and past-life curses, but you can work toward resolving them through deep reflection, meditation, and self-awareness.

7. Yourself

In psychic practice, your well-being can sometimes be compromised by your actions or lack thereof. Low self-esteem, a lack of awareness, distorted boundaries, unresolved emotions, personal fears, and critical self-judgments can contribute to psychic attack scenarios. Fearful individuals might see malevolent entities lurking in the shadows, while angry people see everyone as hostile and seeking to do them harm. The world around you is a mirror, and you inadvertently become your own enemy, sabotaging yourself. Rather than placing blame elsewhere, it is important to introspect, realize you could be involved, and take responsibility for your actions.

Psychic protection is an essential aspect of spiritual practice and everyday life. The world is filled with different energies, and not all are positive. Your thoughts, emotions, and interactions with others can leave you vulnerable to harmful energies manifesting as physical, mental, or emotional discomfort. Therefore, protecting yourself from negative energies is crucial to maintaining your well-being and living a balanced life.

Chapter 2: Prepare Your Psyche First

Now that you understand the significance of psychic protection and negative energies' impact on your life, take the first step to protect yourself against these vibes. However, before you start, you must prepare your psyche first. This chapter covers multiple techniques to raise your vibration and sharpen your psychic skills to prepare for various cleansing and protection rituals.

Raising Your Vibrations

Taking yoga classes can help raise your vibration.
https://pixabay.com/sv/photos/yoga-utomhus-soluppg%C3%A5ng-meditation-6723315/

The energy particles in your body are constantly moving and vibrating at a specific rhythm. Your mood and mindset impact the frequency of your vibrations. Positive emotions like gratitude, happiness, and peacefulness can raise your vibes, while negative ones like fear, anxiety, and anger lower their frequency. In other words, attracting positivity into your life increases your vibrations. You will feel lighter spiritually, emotionally, and physically when you vibrate at a higher frequency, while low vibes make you feel heavy and stressed.

Sometimes, it can be hard to control your emotions, especially if your work or home life is stressful. However, a few things can calm your thoughts, relax your body to attract positive vibes and connect you with everything and everyone in the universe.

Move Your Body

You have probably heard about the many benefits of working out, walking, and yoga, but do you know they can raise your vibrations? Moving your body increases the levels of chemicals like dopamine, serotonin, and endorphins helping you to relax and improve your mood. Moving your body reduces harmful hormones like cortisol and adrenaline that make you stressed and anxious.

You don't have to do intense exercises or go to the gym daily; swimming, dancing, riding a bike, walking in nature, hula hooping, jumping a rope, or taking a yoga class will do the trick. It doesn't matter what you do as long as you constantly move your body.

Listen to Music

Everyone knows music makes you feel good and improves your mood. Listen to songs that energize and uplift you while getting ready in the morning or on your way to work. Sing along or dance to the music, and you will feel your vibes rising.

Repeat Affirmations

Affirmations are positive statements that influence your subconscious and conscious mind to think positively. Repeating affirmations can alter your mood, change your mindset, and boost your confidence. However, they will only work if you believe in yourself and what you say and repeat them daily.

Create your own affirmations or repeat these statements to raise your vibrations.

- I am a highly vibrational human.
- I feel at peace.
- I am full of energy.
- I am a magnet that only attracts positive vibes.
- I am thankful to be healthy.
- I am raising my vibration.
- I create my life.
- I love the person I have become.
- I am surrounded by positivity.
- I vibrate higher and feel lighter.
- I embrace all the high-vibe experiences coming my way.
- I am grateful and happy with my life.
- I am vibrating at a high frequency.
- I choose gratitude and happiness every day.
- I am in harmony with the universe.
- I deserve all the good things in life.
- I choose gratitude and joy every day.
- I choose to love and have positive energy.
- I am in control of my life.
- I am raising my vibes.
- I attract positive experiences and people.
- I only think positively.
- I give joy and receive positivity and happiness.
- I witness miracles every day.
- I have everything I need.
- I spread positivity wherever I go.
- I manifest my desires through my high vibrations.
- I choose to raise my vibes every day.

Aromatherapy

Aromatherapy is using essential oils to improve your well-being and health. It is an ancient holistic treatment people still use today. Some scents can impact your brain and influence your emotions. For instance, smelling lavender oil can relax you and reduce stress. Frankincense, chamomile, and eucalyptus are known for their calming effects. Smelling citrus and peppermint can improve your mood and raise your vibration.

You can use an oil diffuser to spread the scent in your home, apply diluted oils on your wrists or behind your earlobe, or use scented candles in the room where you are.

Daily Routine

Many people associate having a daily routine with boredom, but it can be effective in raising your vibration. If you set time aside each day to do something you enjoy, you will have something to look forward to. For example, morning coffee or walking in nature can be great choices. Be sure to incorporate things that bring joy into your daily routine. Even if it's something small like eating chocolate, it will make your day extra special.

Plants

Bring nature into your home if you don't have a garden or live away from nature. Place a few plant pots in different areas in your house. They will improve the décor, reduce stress, make you feel relaxed, clean the air, improve your mood, and raise your vibration.

Journaling

Many thoughts go through your head that can cause stress and anxiety and lower your vibrations. Putting these thoughts on paper is a great way to clear your head and come face-to-face with whatever is troubling you. Often, when you write down your fears and read them out loud, you will realize they aren't as serious as your mind has made them out to be.

Every night before you go to sleep, sit down and write every thought in your journal, whether these are issues you are dealing with or goals you wish to achieve. Organize and prioritize them, and develop a plan to solve your problems or accomplish your goals.

If you are new to journaling and looking for things to write to raise your vibration, tackle these questions:

- How can you add value to your life and the world?
- What nourishes your body, mind, and spirit?

- How do you practice self-love and self-care?
- What makes you get up in the morning and why?
- What makes you the proudest?
- When and where do you feel happiest?
- Describe your ideal day and what you can do to achieve this feeling.

Practice Gratitude

Being grateful for your blessings and focusing on what you have rather than what's missing can change your outlook and raise your vibration. Practicing gratitude can be challenging for some as they struggle to find things to be grateful for every day. However life is full of many gifts you can be thankful for, but they are usually small things you often don't notice or you take for granted, like not facing traffic on your way to work, having a perfect cup of coffee, or getting a hug from your neighbor's dog.

Write down the things you are thankful for, but instead of making a list like "I am grateful for my children" or "I am grateful for my health," explain why you appreciate them, what makes them special, how they make your life better, and how you would feel without them. Daily, write one thing you are grateful for with three to five reasons why they are significant. By the time you have finished, you will feel better, and your vibes will rise. Whenever you feel low, you can always turn to your gratitude journal to remember all your blessings, and your mood will instantly change.

Socialize

Even the most introverted people need to connect with others and feel part of a community; it's human nature. Spend time with people who lift you up and make you feel better about yourself. Choose ones you share common interests and values with and can talk to about anything. Stay away from people who lower your vibes by judging you, making you feel bad about yourself, and reminding you of your past failures rather than supporting and celebrating your successes. Look at your circle and notice who raises your energy after spending time with them and who brings you down and drains you. Positivity is infectious, so surround yourself with people from whom you can catch positive vibes.

Reiki

Reiki is a healing technique where a practitioner uses their hand to transfer positive energy to your body to reduce stress and make you feel relaxed. During a reiki session, the practitioner will loosen negative energy and clear your pathways to raise vibrations.

Disconnect

In this modern age, people are always online and behind their screens, usually checking their friends and family's pictures on Instagram, and can't help but compare their lives with those of their friends. It leads to negative thoughts and low vibes. Disconnect for a few hours every day and connect with yourself. Do something you love and practice self-care, like a massage, reading a book, cooking a healthy meal, trying something new, or finishing a project you have been procrastinating on. Simply slow down, focus on the present, and enjoy the moment.

Be Creative

When was the last time you did a creative project? Unfortunately, many people don't have the time to create or have been discouraged. Do something you are passionate about to spend hours on and lose yourself in it. You will feel less stressed, more confident, and in a better mood after you finish. These feelings usually result from dopamine released in your body when you feel accomplished and proud of something you created.

If you can't find something you are passionate about, think back to your childhood. What did you enjoy doing? Or maybe there is something you have always wanted to try, like painting, singing, or writing. When you find it, start creating.

Be in Nature

Nature is the closest thing humans have to magic. Walking or hiking while being surrounded by beautiful scenery can alter your mood and vibes. The sunlight on your face, the wind in your hair, and the ground beneath your feet can make you feel relaxed and at peace.

Declutter

Nothing says low vibration more than clutter. Messy environments drain your energy and make you feel stressed and uncomfortable. Many of these unnecessary items can carry negative energies or memories to make you unhappy. Remove everything you no longer need to allow easy energy flow in your home. Keep what you use, make yourself happy, and add meaning to your life. Donate your clutter instead of throwing it away, making this process more meaningful.

Get to the Root of the Negativity

Dig deep into yourself to determine the reason behind the negative energy and emotions you have been experiencing. Journaling and therapy can push you to get real with yourself, confront your feelings to get to the root of your problem, fix it, and raise your vibes.

Love Yourself

Treat yourself with love and compassion. Use positive words when you talk about yourself, and avoid negative thoughts. Imagine a loved one feeling low and coming to you for support. What would you tell them? Use this same kindness on yourself whenever you feel sad and need encouragement.

Forgive and Forget

Holding grudges can make you feel heavy, consume you with negative emotions, and lower your vibes. It's time to forgive and forget. Either forgive the ones who hurt you and turn over a new leaf or let them go and move on from everything they put you through, releasing the negative energy and replacing it with positive energy.

What matters the most is forgiving yourself. Don't spend your life in regrets and self-blame. Understand you are human, and making mistakes is normal; it's how you learn.

Meditation

Meditation is one of the most effective tools against low vibes. It looks inward and focuses on positive emotions and letting go of the chaos and negative energy impacting your vibration. Meditation is like decluttering your brain and spirit as you let go of the thoughts and emotions no longer benefiting you and embrace positive and calming ones. You can meditate at home after you wake up, before bed, or even at work. You only need ten or fifteen minutes daily, making a huge difference in your life.

Meditation Technique
Instructions:

1. Choose a quiet room or space with no distractions, and set your phone to silent. You can play soft music if you prefer.

2. Sit straight, place your hands on your knees with your palms facing up, and ensure you are comfortable.
3. Close your eyes, clear your mind, and focus on the present moment.
4. Breathe deeply through your nose and out through your mouth a few times.
5. Feel the stress, anxiety, and negativity leave your body with every breath you take and exhale.
6. Focus on your breathing and feel the air entering and leaving your chest. You are inhaling positivity and relaxation and exhaling negative vibes.
7. Visualize yourself surrounded by white light. This light is the calming, loving, and healing energy raising your vibration.
8. Feel the light nourish and energize your body, mind, and spirit with every breath.
9. Feel positive emotions like love, joy, gratitude, kindness, compassion, or other feelings you experience in that moment.
10. Sit with these feelings for a while, then end the session by expressing gratitude.

Visualization

Visualizing is imagining something you want to attract into your life. Even though you only visualize the moment and aren't living it, you can still experience all its positive emotions.

Visualization Technique
Instructions:
1. Sit or lie in a quiet room, whatever makes you comfortable.
2. Close your eyes and slowly breathe until you feel relaxed and calm.
3. Visualize a moment or a place that makes you happy. It can also be a place you hope to visit.
4. Experience the moment in your imagination with each of your five senses. Focus on what you hear, like your mother's or children's voices. Focus on the scents around you, like flowers, your grandma's favorite recipe, or the ocean. What

are you feeling? Is it a cold winter night or a warm summer day? Look around your image and take in everything you see, like the stars, moon, flowers, or your loved ones' faces.

5. Now, imagine yourself moving around and feeling more peaceful and joyful.
6. Keep breathing slowly and taking in your surroundings while experiencing them with each of your five senses.
7. Imagine positive vibes and harmony entering your body and the negative vibes leaving with every breath.
8. To finish your visualization session, slowly open your eyes and continue breathing until you are ready to move.

Breathing

Whatever you face in life, you always remind yourself to breathe. Breathing can soothe your body and mind to calm you down whenever you are stressed, anxious, or scared. Various breathing exercises can raise your vibration.

Breathing Technique
Nadi Shodhana

Nadi Shodhana is a breathing exercise referred to as alternate-nostril breathing. Practice breathing exercises like meditation and visualization by sitting comfortably in a quiet space.

Instructions:

1. Use your ring finger and thumb to block each of your nostrils.
2. Breathe in through your left nostril while blocking your right one, then block the left nostril and breathe out through the right. Reverse the process by blocking your right nostril and breathing in through the left one.
3. Repeat the process a few times and prolong the inhaling and exhaling until you feel relaxed.

Sharpen Your Psychic Skills

Protecting yourself from psychic attacks involves soul cleansing and summoning your guardian angel, which you can only do by tapping into your intuition and sharpening your skills. These skills will push you to go beyond the physical and into the spiritual world.

Listen to Your Gut

Never ignore your gut feeling because it's usually right. If someone or something makes you feel uncomfortable or even sick, this is your intuition telling you to assess the situation since something isn't right. Everyone has an inner voice, but only a few connect with and experience it. Stay attuned to this voice; when it warns you against something, take it seriously.

Use Your Five Senses

Process information and feel everything around you using your five senses. You will probably see and hear things other people don't, but you won't notice them without employing all your senses.

Be Prepared

When you sharpen your psychic skills, you begin to receive various messages. However, some will not make sense. Believe that whatever you see is real, even if it's something simple like an object or a name. You can only sharpen your skills by taking every message you receive seriously. You will experience negative energies since you are open and ready to receive anything that comes to you. Teach yourself not to pay attention to negativity by letting it flow through you or practice any techniques to raise your vibration.

Throughout your life, you will attract all energy forms. When your psychic skills are sharpened, it leaves you open to good and harmful vibes. Raising your vibration protects you against negativity. The techniques in this chapter should become a part of your daily routine to act as a weapon against the negative energies you constantly receive. Eventually, practicing these techniques becomes habitual, and your intuition and vibrations will automatically alert you to harmful energies against you, your family, and your loved ones. When you are experienced and confident using these techniques, teach them to those you deeply care about, so they can gain the same protection, positivity, and happiness as you.

Remember, positivity attracts good vibes, and negativity attracts bad ones. When you replace emotions like sadness and anger with joy and gratitude, you invite good things into your life, raising your vibration and preparing you for cleansing your karma and soul.

Chapter 3: Soul and Karma Cleansing

Like you take precautions to maintain good health, prevention techniques are the most effective way to approach psychic defense issues. This approach aims to restore balance and harmony, which can help prevent disturbances that can throw you off center. Regular spiritual cleansing practice can strengthen you to withstand psychic attacks better, leaving you less vulnerable to harm. These basic psychic care forms can help you develop psychic immunity to most forms of harm and provide protection against external negative influences.

Soul and karma cleansing can help restore your life's balance.
https://www.pexels.com/photo/a-golden-balance-scale-beside-a-laptop-6077797/

You've studied the concept of energy bodies in the previous chapters and are now aware of how they can affect your overall well-being. Caring for your energy body is just as important as caring for your physical hygiene. Like you prevent physical bacteria from accumulating and consuming life-giving substances for your physical body, you must do the same for your spiritual body. Your day-to-day interactions leave your energy body unbalanced and contaminated.

Although many believe they only have one body with an animating force known as the soul, true psychic individuals recognize that humans have different energy bodies making up their unique blend of energies. Metaphysicians categorize these energy bodies differently. Some systems have seven, nine, ten, or twelve bodies, each with unique attributes. However, regardless of the name or culture, these more complex systems can usually be simplified down to four bodies based on the four elements. Each body has specific needs and methods of care and cleansing, and each element offers its path to psychic hygiene on various levels.

The techniques for elemental hygiene overlap in purpose and execution since the spiritual bodies interpenetrate each other. Finding at least one technique that resonates with you and using it often is important. Each body's health is dependent on the health of the others. Changes in one body affect all the others, from the subtlest to the denser levels and back again, so you shouldn't neglect the cleansing process of any energy body. Below are in-depth explanations of how each energy body works, what role it plays, and how you can cleanse them from external energy contamination:

The Physical Body

The physical body is probably the easiest concept to grasp. It consists of flesh, blood, organs, and bones. The physical body is associated with the earth element, considered the densest of all four elements. So, the most powerful and earthy cleansing techniques are required for the spiritual cleansing of the physical body. These techniques include simple rituals with straightforward physical actions and can have a far-reaching effect on all your energy bodies. The most common cleansing ritual is smudging, a simple but powerful ritual that many people do almost daily.

Smudging is passing yourself, others, or objects through the sacred smoke of a blessed incense. The smoke is believed to purify and cleanse the person or object energetically. Although smudging is mostly used to cleanse a space or object, it can cleanse people. The materials used in smudging, like woods, herbs, and resins, are derived from the natural world, i.e., organic and in harmony with the earth element. When burned, the materials' vibration intensifies and is released into the intended space, emanating much further than the visible smoke. It is further intensified when the incense is blessed.

People refer to lower, slower, and more stagnant energies when discussing "negative" or harmful energy. Burning a powerfully protective and cleansing incense forces these lower vibrations to match or be removed from the area, as they cannot exist at that lower, dense level when surrounded by refined energy. The higher energy entrains the lower energy to match it; if it cannot, it must leave the sacred space.

Instructions for Smudging

Various incense forms are available, including wands, cones, sticks, and granules. Smudge wands are bundles of dried herbs tightly packed together. Although these can be purchased commercially, it can be fun to make them yourself. Gather fresh herbs and lay them together. Wrap them tightly with cotton string and allow them to dry evenly on a screen. Then light the tip and blow it out to create sacred smoke. Ensure you have a flameproof vessel to hold under the smudge stick, such as an earthen bowl or seashell.

Powdered incense is messier but provides a more "witchy" vibe. Grind your herbs to a powder using a traditional mortar and pestle or an electric grinder. Then, get some charcoal blocks or discs, commonly sold in stores, to use as your combustible base. Light the charcoal and sprinkle the incense on it to burn, adding more incense occasionally if you need more smoke. Use a nonflammable utensil to brush off the accumulated ash and add more herbs.

Once the incense is smoking, pass whatever objects you are clearing through the smoke. When smudging yourself, waft the smoke all over your body, including the front and back. Feathers, like turkey or crow feathers, are often used with traditional sage wands or other herb bundles to fan the embers and create more smoke.

Smudging can be ceremonial. Hold the burning incense to the north, east, south, west, above, below near the ground, left side, right side, and then the heart, asking for the blessing of all the directions and gods before smudging yourself, someone else, or an object. Being present and aware of your body is essential to truly protect the physical body. Center yourself through rituals like smudging. By being aware, you react more effectively to difficult situations.

The Emotional Body

The emotional body is known by different names, which include the astral body, psychic body, and dream body. Symbolized by the water element, it flows and takes shape like water in a vessel, with the force of imagination and willpower giving it form. When you connect with them during your sleep, your thoughts, hopes, dreams, and fears take shape on the astral plane. Similarly, your emotions take on shape and form, flow easily like water, and are susceptible to emotional pollutants and toxins from others if you lack strong boundaries.

Empathy is the ability to feel and relate to someone else's emotions and points of view. An energy can be a blessing or a curse depending on how it is expressed and handled. It is a great gift when you are solid in your personal foundation and use your sensitivity to gain greater awareness of relationships and situations. Those with healthy empathy often become healers, teachers, therapists, social workers, artists, performers, and musicians.

However, uncontrolled empathy can be overwhelming and confusing, and without strong boundaries, it is hard to discern which feelings come from an outside source and which are yours. Regular, disciplined meditation and rituals of an introspective nature, with boundary and healing techniques, are helpful for those with strong empathy issues.

Setting boundaries is key to managing empathic abilities, including shielding yourself from the emotional energy of others and recognizing when to step back and focus on your emotional well-being. Regularly practicing self-care to avoid burnout and becoming overwhelmed is important.

In addition to empathy, other forms of psychic sensitivity affect the emotional body. These include clairvoyance, clairaudience, and clairsentience, among others. Each of these abilities has a different way of perceiving psychic information and uniquely impacts the emotional body.

Developing and honing these abilities can be a valuable tool for understanding and navigating the emotional landscape of yourself and others. However, approaching these abilities with responsibility and discernment and seeking guidance and support is crucial.

Ritual Bathing

Ritual bathing is a powerful technique to cleanse and heal the emotional body. The purifying qualities of water should not be underestimated. While many witchcraft traditions emphasize the importance of a ritual bath before serious workings, most witches skip the bath and jump straight into spells. However, when engaging in a ritual bath, the ritual has a more charged, more psychic, and more magnetic quality. Water has the ability to cleanse the emotional and physical body, and using protective and cleansing herbs in ritual baths infuses the water with their properties. Salts draw out dense energies, and vinegar neutralizes harmful energies. For example, vinegar can be left in a bowl to absorb and collect harmful energies and then discarded into the earth or down a drain.

Here is a cleansing bath salt recipe with a mix of sea salt, lavender flowers or leaves, yarrow flowers or leaves, mugwort or myrrh, and lavender and myrrh essential oil.

1. Mix the ingredients together while holding each one (except for the oils) in your hands, allowing your energy to mingle with the natural healing powers of each ingredient.
2. When the ingredients are mixed, place the mixture in an airtight bottle for a few weeks to allow the scents to mingle.
3. Place a few tablespoons of the mixture in a muslin or cotton bag and submerge it in the bath water.
4. When ready to get out of the bath, allow the water to drain while sitting in the tub. It allows unwanted energies to go down the drain and be neutralized with salt and herbs.

Floral Rituals

Another water-based protection method is using herbal and floral waters - rose water is the most common and powerful. Rose water can be bought at drug stores or made at home using rose essential oil, water, and alcohol. The number of essential oil drops varies depending on the preferred strength of the scent. Another method for making rose water is making a tea infusion of rose petals and water, then mixing it with the water and alcohol solution. A true hydrosol can be created using a large pot, two smaller bowls, and a cover with rose petals and water. The water collected in the bowl is your rose water, known as rose hydrosol, which should be preserved with alcohol or glycerin.

Roses are spiritually uplifting and grounding and are considered the vibration of pure love. They are the most protective substance in many traditions. The flower symbolizes love, while the thorns symbolize protection. If rose water or oil is unavailable, you can visualize roses around you for protection, inviting the rose flower's spirit, which wilts in the mind's eye as it absorbs harmful energy.

The Mental Body

The mind is the body, often requiring the most cleansing. Typically, the mind is chaotic and cluttered, making it difficult to find and utilize useful information without being hindered by accumulated waste from the past. Consequently, the spiritual process is primarily about eliminating excess baggage from your mental closet to establish harmony and order. While generating millions of thoughts daily, the majority are repeated, following familiar, static patterns and rarely creating anything new. Thoughts are less dense and create feelings, while emotions are denser than thoughts. Focusing on a thought long enough can conjure up associated feelings creating sensations and bodily reactions measurable in the physical world. The physical world is denser than the emotional world. Therefore, the state of mind determines health at the emotional and physical levels.

True innovators and magical individuals can think beyond the usual patterns and habits to see things differently. The mental bodies must be trained similarly to physical bodies. Traditional school work, like math and memorization, is helpful but not the most powerful technique, as it can trap the mind into patterns. Mental cleansing is not about thinking like everyone else but about discovering your true self. The most mentally cleansing experiences are those eliminating what does not serve the mind and helping train the mind to be a tool, servant, and aid instead of the master. Mental introspection is the key, which brings awareness to the habits and patterns contributing to undesirable events in your life.

Journaling is an excellent starting point for introspective work. Writing down the things in your mind establishes discipline and enables you to identify patterns consciously. Keeping a dream journal to help reflect on the subconscious themes manifested in sleep is essential.

Regular meditation is another tool for mental hygiene. It involves taking time to be quiet and listen to your highest guidance. Various meditation techniques are available, such as Eastern techniques of watching the mind, focusing on the breath, or using a mantra, and Western visualization and relaxation techniques. Regular meditation reduces stress, increases vitality, and enhances creativity.

The Soul Body

The soul body is connected to the fire element, representing the personal spark of divinity within everyone. The soul is often referred to as the higher self and is associated with the highest level of spiritual knowledge. It is the most energetic and elusive part of yourself and, therefore, the most protected and untouchable from external harm. The fiery nature of the soul prevents the accumulation of harmful energy, burning away that which doesn't serve you in a positive way. You achieve true protection, fearlessness, and eternal wisdom by identifying with the soul rather than the mind, emotions, or body. In true essence, you are connected to all things yet bound by none.

The techniques for healing and protection use fire to extend divine energy from the soul into other subtle bodies. The first technique is getting in touch with solar fire directly by going outside into the sunlight for five to ten minutes daily. It allows the Sun's spiritual energy to burn harmful energies that could have accumulated and fill your aura with vital life energy, making you healthier and more resistant to harm. The second technique is visualizing the Sun while in meditation and drawing down the Sun's golden white light to surround and revitalize you.

You must think of yourself as existing on all four spiritual levels simultaneously and seek balance and harmony with your physical, emotional, mental, and soul components to achieve true health. Mastery of these levels provides spiritual protection, so you don't have to be in a deep trance or perform an in-depth ritual to invite the healing energies of fire, light, and the Sun for health and protection.

Understanding Karma

The concept of karma is not complex or abstract. It refers to your actions and the consequences that arise from them. Karma is a cycle of cause and effect that shapes lives. Your past actions influence your present and future experiences. Positive actions create love-based karma, which brings valuable lessons for personal growth. In contrast, negative actions create fear-based karma, often leading to judgment and consequences. However, negative karma can be transformed into positive by showing love, compassion, and forgiveness to yourself and others.

Maintaining purity in thoughts, words, and actions is essential to create good karma. Despite your best intentions, sometimes you cause pain or hurt. In these situations, acknowledging your mistakes, learning from them, and making amends is crucial. Forgiving yourself and others to prevent negative energy from returning is vital.

You must send love and light to everyone, avoid hidden motives or control dramas, cultivate gratitude, and practice forgiveness to create positive karma. Forgiveness is a challenging but essential practice to manifest love-based karma. Guilt and negative emotions can lead to unnecessary suffering, but you can move forward and grow by forgiving yourself and others. Remember, mistakes are part of being human, and you can always learn from them.

Further Techniques for Cleansing the Soul

- **Sound healing:** Sound healing uses sound frequencies to balance the mind, body, and soul. It uses instruments like singing bowls, gongs, or tuning forks to produce vibrations penetrating the body and help release blocked energy. You can attend a sound healing session with a practitioner or perform it at home by playing soothing music and focusing on the vibrations.

- **Chakra cleansing:** Chakras are energy centers in the body that can become blocked or imbalanced, leading to physical and emotional issues. Chakra cleansing uses various techniques to release blockages and balance the energy flow. Techniques can include visualization, meditation, or crystals.

- **Breathwork:** Breathwork uses specific breathing techniques to access different states of consciousness and release stored emotions or trauma. It can be done with a practitioner or at home using guided breathwork meditations.

- **Forest Bathing:** Forest Bathing, known as *shinrin-yoku*, is a Japanese practice of immersing yourself in nature and using all your senses to connect with the environment. It can help reduce stress and anxiety, boost mood, and promote calm and relaxation.

- **Cord Cutting**: Cord cutting is a visualization technique of cutting energetic cords between yourself and another person or situation. It can help you to release negative energy, let go of past traumas, and create healthy boundaries.
- **Shamanic Journeying:** Shamanic journeying uses rhythmic drumming or other sounds to enter into an altered state of consciousness. During this state, you can connect with your inner wisdom, spirit guides, and other sources of guidance and healing.

Soul and karma cleansing are vital practices for anyone seeking a balanced and fulfilling life. Your actions, thoughts, and emotions create your karma, affecting you and those around you. Purifying your soul and clearing karmic debts aligns you with a higher purpose and living in harmony with the universe. It is not always an easy journey, and setbacks will occur, but with dedication, patience, and perseverance, you can transform and positively impact the world. Remember, the power to cleanse your soul and karma lies within you. It is never too late to start. So, take the first step today, and begin your journey toward a brighter future.

Chapter 4: Cleansing Your Space and Others

Past energies and influences attach themselves to people and places. For instance, if you fought with your spouse in your living room, the space would be filled with negativity that won't disappear until you perform a cleansing ritual. For this reason, people usually purify their homes after a divorce, bad breakup, or financial trouble to remove the impact of these negative experiences. Cleansing an area is similar to pressing a reset button, turning it back to its original high frequency before negative energy impacts its vibration.

Cleansing your space will clear the negative energy surrounding it.
https://www.pexels.com/photo/a-woman-holding-a-sage-with-smoke-6628539/

Cleansing your home is necessary before performing spiritual or energy work. Even if you haven't experienced negativity, you should still cleanse the place at least once a week because you never know what negative vibes your or your family members have brought in recently. Clearing negative energy frees space for positive vibes to enter your home and life.

It is similar to getting the flu. After you recover, you usually wash your linens and clothes and take a shower to wash away the germs. You open the windows to clear your home from sickly vibes and allow energy to flow. Afterward, you feel lighter and better. The same happens when you cleanse a room. You will feel the space's vibe changing, impacting your mood.

Since people and objects vibrate in different frequencies, lower vibes usually rise slightly to meet higher frequencies. However, high vibration drops so the two can meet in the middle. For instance, bringing a crystal to your unclean space will raise the area's frequency, but the crystal's vibe will lower to match the surrounding energy.

Keep your space protected by constantly performing purification rituals, especially after you have guests, to clear the impact of their energy. Regular cleansing makes it easier to eliminate unwanted vibrations before they cause serious damage.

If you want to raise protection around a specific space, ensure it is free of lingering negative energy. You can tell a room has low vibration from the moment you enter because you will feel uncomfortable or tense immediately. Check the place's energy before you begin working, even if you have recently cleansed it. Your spouse or a family member could have had an argument at home and lowered its vibe.

Negative Energy in Your Home

You are probably wondering if your home has negative energy or not. Often, you can sense these vibes in the room, but if you are stressed or anxious, it can be hard to separate your negative emotions from the house's vibes. However, there are certain signs to look out for indicating negative energy in your home is affecting you and your family.

Bad Relationships

Look at the relationship of everyone in the house. Are you constantly arguing with your spouse? Are your children always fighting with one another? Do you feel your relationship with your family is strained? It could result in negative vibes in your home.

Constant Complaining

There is no denying that life is stressful, and you can catch yourself occasionally complaining about your work, your terrible boss, or the traffic. However, if you and your family constantly complain - even when things are going well - and you can't find the good in life, your home requires cleansing.

Excessive Blame

If everyone in your home is always blaming and criticizing each other and refusing to take responsibility for their actions, this could be the impact of negative vibes.

Clutter

Clutter doesn't only lower your vibes, but it also spreads negative energy around your home. Crowded furniture and mess can create a chaotic environment. Your furniture should be arranged so it allows energy to flow easily around the house,

Cleansing a space is very simple. You can do many weekly or daily rituals that won't take much time or effort.

This chapter covers various rituals to purify your home, altar, or other spaces.

Declutter and Clean Your Home

Remove all the items you don't need and vacuum and dust every corner of your home. Don't keep broken items like a cracked vase because they invite negative vibes. After decluttering, cleanse the house with this purifying solution you can easily make at home.

Ingredients:

- 1 cup of sea salt
- 5 lemons
- ¼ cup of white vinegar

Instructions:

1. Fill a bucket with water, add the sea salt and white vinegar, then squeeze in the lemons.
2. Using a towel, clean the window, frames, doors, and doorknobs.

Build an Altar

Altars are the perfect place for spiritual work but can also release negative energy or invite positive energy.

Instructions:
1. Set the altar in the space where you will perform your spiritual work.
2. Set an intention for the altar, like inviting positive energy into your home.
3. Clean the area by removing the dust and decluttering the space.
4. Place various objects symbolizing protection, abundance, good health, good fortune, and prosperity. In other words, add objects representing the energy you want in your home.
5. Add crystals, flowers, pictures, statues, candles, incense, or other objects that bring you comfort and happiness.
6. Organize all the items on your altar and avoid cluttering it or the space around it.

Smudge Ritual #1

Burning herbs is one of the oldest cleansing rituals. The Native Americans used it for centuries to cleanse themselves and their homes of negative energy. This ritual's recipe includes multiple dried herbs, but you can use only a couple if you prefer.

Ingredients:
- Basil
- Pine cones
- Cloves
- Lavender
- Rosemary
- Juniper
- Sweetgrass
- Cedar
- Palo santo

- Garden sage
- White sage

Instructions:

1. Open the house windows to allow the negative energy to escape.
2. Set an intention of what you hope to achieve from this ritual, like cleansing your home of negative vibes, or think of mantras and affirmations, like *"I am cleansing this room of negative energy to free space for love and light."*
3. Wrap the herbs in a bundle and light them at one end until they release smoke.
4. Gently fan the smoke with your hand, then move clockwise around the room to cleanse the desired space while repeating the intention.

Smudge Ritual #2

Ingredients and Tools:

- Sage with dragon blood or white sage
- A candle
- Incense (choose your favorite scent)
- A ceramic dish for the incense
- Sweetgrass essential oil

Instructions:

1. Organize and declutter the space before you begin the ritual, then open the windows.
2. Burn the sage and move clockwise around the room while thinking about the positive vibes you want to surround yourself with and what you plan to do with the cleansed space.
3. Put the sage on a dish, place it in the center of your home, and leave it to burn.
4. Now you have released the negative energy and freed space to welcome positive vibes.
5. Sweetgrass can attract positive energy, so apply 10 to 20 drops of sweetgrass essential oil in a diffuser. It is more

effective to use it directly after the sage.

Spray Ritual

Ingredients and Tools:
- Essential oils (use any oils you prefer)
- Pure alcohol
- Distilled water
- Spray bottle (glass or plastic)

Instructions:
1. Pour 50 ml of water into an empty glass, then add 20 drops of essential oils.
2. Mix the alcohol with the water.
3. Pour the mixture into a diffuser or a spray bottle, then spray the room you wish to cleanse while repeating your intention.

Burn Ritual

Tools:
- Paper
- Pen
- Candle
- Crystal
- Cinnamon stick

Instructions:
1. Write down what you hope to achieve from this cleansing ritual on the piece of paper, fold it, and place it in front of you.
2. Light the candle and use it to light your cinnamon stick.
3. Place the cinnamon stick and the crystal on the area you want to cleanse and leave them for a few minutes (keep your eyes on the cinnamon stick because it can be a fire hazard).
4. Burn the piece of paper in the candle.

Salt Ritual

In some cultures, salt symbolizes purity and can cleanse an area of negative energy and raise its vibes.

Ingredients:

- Salt

Instructions:

1. Pour a small amount of salt into a bowl and place it at your front door to prevent negative energy from entering your home.
2. Remove the objects from the area you want to cleanse, dust the corners, and sprinkle salt around the room.
3. Ensure the salt remains undisturbed for a couple of days, so keep children and pets away from the room.

Tuning Fork Ritual

Ancient cultures used the power of sound and music to heal different ailments. In ancient Greece, physicians used singing bowls, instruments, and vibrations as sound therapy to treat insomnia. Certain sound frequencies can clear the air from negative energy caused by stress and tension.

Tools:

- Tuning fork

Instructions:

1. Sit in a comfortable position.
2. Set an intention for cleansing your area and renewing the energy.
3. Gently tap the tuning fork against a table or solid space.
4. Close your eyes and feel the sound vibrating in every area around the room.
5. Repeat the process until you feel the vibes in the room rising.

Bell Ritual

Since sound can be an effective weapon against negative energy, you can use other methods like ringing a bell. Ring a bell in different rooms around your home, and the vibration will spread across the house, releasing negative energy.

Visualization Ritual

Instructions:

1. Sit in a quiet room without distractions and relax your body and mind.
2. Close your eyes and take deep and slow breaths.
3. Imagine a ball of golden light floating next to your heart.
4. The light keeps expanding with every breath until it exits your body.
5. Spread the light around the area you wish to cleanse while setting an intention.
6. When you have finished, slowly open your eyes and express your gratitude.

Lemon Ritual

Have you ever wondered why many cleaning products contain lemon as their main ingredient? Lemon's scent is uplifting and can alter the energy of the room.

Tips:

- Put 20 drops of lemon essential oil in a diffuser and place it in the room you want to cleanse.
- Cut lemons into slices and put them in a few bowls in different corners around the house.
- Simmer lemon peels and let the steam fill the house.

Water Ritual

Ingredients:

- Water
- Orange blossom water, rose water, or your favorite essential oil

Instructions:
1. Pour filtered water into a bucket and add 2 to 5 drops of essential oil, rose water, or orange blossom water.
2. Add cleaning soap to the bucket and cleanse your floors, windows, and front door.

Reiki Ritual

You don't need a practitioner for this ritual; you can do it yourself at home.

Instructions:
1. Sit in a comfortable position and close your eyes.
2. Breathe deeply and focus on your breath.
3. Visualize healing white light flowing into you from your head, then into your body, and exiting through your hands.
4. Feel the healing power inside you, filling you with loving and positive energy.
5. Release this healing energy through your hands into the room
6. When you finish, express your gratitude for the healing energy.

Crystals Ritual

Tools:
- Smoky quartz
- Onyx
- Black tourmaline

Instructions:
1. Place these crystals in the room or space you wish to cleanse and leave them for a few days.
2. Afterward, cleanse the crystals from the negative energy by leaving them overnight under the moonlight.

Open Windows

Fresh air can clear negative energy from your home and replace it with positive vibes. Open all your windows and allow the fresh air to fill the place. You can turn on the fans to allow air circulation and open your drawers and closets to release stagnant energy.

Repaint Your Walls

Look at your house's walls. If the colors are dark or dull and make you feel stressed or down, it is time for some interior design. Repaint the walls with a bright color or apply an interesting wallpaper. You can add wall art and other decoration to liven the place and release negative vibes.

Cleansing Your Children

You love no one more than your child and want to protect them from harm. It is hard for a parent to believe their kid is exposed to negative energy. However, children can experience stress, anxiety, and toxic vibes daily. Although you can't shield them from the world, you can prevent the negativity from ruining their lives. Certain techniques can cleanse your little one from negative energy.

Visualization

You have learned that visualization is a powerful technique against negative energy. Similar to using this method to raise your vibe and purify your home, you can use it to cleanse your child from negative energy. However, they cannot do this technique themselves, so you must do it for them.

Instructions:

1. Sit in a quiet room in a comfortable position and close your eyes.
2. Visualize white protective light wrapping your child.
3. Spend a few minutes focusing on this image, slowly open your eyes, and express your gratitude.

Spinal Flush

Perform this technique on your child after they have been exposed to negative situations or people.

Instructions:

1. Place your hand on the top of your child's spine between the shoulders and neck.
2. Slowly and gently move your hand down to their tailbone, then up again.

3. Tell your child to take deep breaths while you move your hand.
4. Repeat this motion six times.

Now, teach your child how to protect their energy or "zip it up."
1. Place your hand at the center of your child's front torso.
2. Pretend they are wearing a vest with a zipper that goes up to their chin.
3. Using your hand, pretend you are zipping up the indivisible vest from the bottom to the top.
4. Repeat the motions four times.

Teach your child to do the "zip up" motion. It is a simple and fun exercise they will enjoy doing throughout the day to contain their energy.

Tiny Coal Cure

This method works for a baby or a toddler. Negative energy can impact newborns. If you had guests recently, their negative vibes could rub off on your baby, causing irritability, constant crying, and sickness. Coal cure is an effective treatment to protect your baby against negative energy.

Ingredients and Tools:
- Cold water with 5 ice cubes
- 9 classic matches
- A tall glass

Instructions:
1. Set your intentions and repeat them in a low voice or merely think of them. Don't say them out loud; you should be quiet for this method to work.
2. Pour the water and ice cubes into the tall glass.
3. Light each match above the glass of water and focus on the flame.
4. When half the match is burned, drop it into the water.
5. Count each match and add "not" before the number, like not one, not two, not three, etc.
6. If the matches remain above the water, your child isn't affected by negative energy. If the matches fall to the bottom of the glass, your child has been exposed to bad vibes.

7. Say a little prayer or affirmation to bless the water and use the cure to heal your child from negative energy.
8. Place your fingers in the water and run them across your child's forehead.
9. Dip your fingers and gently rub the sides of their eyes and temples.
10. Dip your fingers in the water and rub their neck to wash away the negativity.
11. Again, dip your fingers and rub their left arm beginning at the shoulder until you reach their fingers. Pretend you are pulling the energy from their body.
12. Repeat the previous step on their right leg.
13. Dip your fingers and move your hand from their belly to their foot.
14. Dip your fingers again and move them down along each leg and pretend you are pulling negative vibes away from them.
15. Pour the remaining water outside your home.
16. You can practice this ritual on children of any age or a loved one, like your parents or spouse.

Protecting Your Pets

Your fur children deserve protection, too. Negative energy can affect pets, especially if your home has bad vibes. Animals are more susceptible to negativity than people since they are more in sync with the universe. These methods can cleanse them from negative energy and keep them protected.

Practice Reiki

Take your pet to a reiki practitioner, or you can do it yourself using the reiki ritual mentioned previously.

Use Crystals

Hang healing crystals on their collar, under their bed, or in water. However, be careful since only a few crystals are safe to put in water, like clear quartz, smokey quartz, or rose quartz. Don't add small stones; your pet will swallow them, so opt for big ones.

Place Spiritual symbols on Your Pet

Place a spiritual symbol on your pet's collar, like the evil eye, OM symbol, or Hamsa Hand, to protect them against negative energy.

Visualization

Employ the same visualization technique you used on your child to cleanse your pet.

You can protect your house, children, pets, and loved ones from the impact of negative energy. The rituals do not have to be complicated and complex to cleanse your home. Regularly repeat these simple and easy rituals to keep your home and family safe.

Chapter 5: Post-Cleanse: Healing Your Aura

You've learned to cleanse your psychic energy and the spaces around you from negative contamination. As you work through the techniques, you'll notice an incredible lightness and clarity within your soul as you shed layers of negativity. However, there's yet another aspect to consider: your aura. Imagine your soul as a freshly cleaned and polished mirror reflecting the purest version of yourself. It reflects your state when you have cleansed and purified your psychic energy.

Auras are energy fields that surround the physical body.
https://pixabay.com/images/id-198958/

But, when you step back into the world, you soon realize the mirror is not as pure as you thought. It's surrounded by a haze of dust, scratches, and smudges. The same is the case for your aura. Even though you've cleansed your energy, your aura can still be contaminated by the negative energy and experiences you've gone through. Each speck of dust and scratch on the surface represents an emotion, experience, or thought that has impacted you. These imprints can distort the reflection of your soul and make it harder to connect with your true self.

The concept of an aura is often dismissed as pseudoscience, but it has been present in various cultures throughout history. The aura can be defined as a subtle energy field surrounding and permeating the physical body, containing information about your physical, emotional, and spiritual state. It is connected to the soul and affected by thoughts, emotions, and experiences. While intangible, it can profoundly impact your well-being and ability to navigate the world around you.

Your aura is a protective shield around you, absorbing and filtering energies from your surroundings. Like any shield, it's prone to wear down over time, leaving you vulnerable to harmful attacks. If your aura is not energized and cleansed, negative energies can seep through the cracks in your protective shield and weaken your aura, making you more susceptible to harm. This damaged aura can manifest as physical, emotional, and mental imbalances if left unchecked. Consequently, giving your aura the attention and care it requires is imperative.

When you cleanse, heal, and strengthen your aura, you ultimately enhance your ability to navigate the world and connect better with your psychic self. But the question is, where do you start? This chapter provides a complete guide to cleansing and healing your aura from the damage inflicted upon it. You can use several techniques, like smudging, crystal healing, or salt baths. You'll learn to restore your aura's balance, remove remnant negative energies, and revitalize your psychic aura. Furthermore, you'll understand the relationship between a healed aura and psychic protection and how a strong aura can enhance your spiritual growth.

What Is an Aura?

An aura is a subtle energy field surrounding and permeating the physical body. It is often described as a luminous field of color seen or felt by sensitive individuals. The aura's purpose is multi-faceted and has been studied by various spiritual traditions and energy healers. One of the aura's primary functions is to protect the physical body from external negative energies. The aura acts as a shield absorbing and filtering out negative energies before they can enter the body. Therefore, many energy healers recommend people take measures to protect their aura, such as wearing protective crystals, practicing meditation, or avoiding negative people or environments.

Another function of the aura is to reflect the state of the body, mind, and soul. The aura's colors, textures, and patterns can change depending on a person's emotional state, physical health, and spiritual well-being. Energy healers use this information to diagnose and treat imbalances within a person's energy field. The aura is also a conduit for spiritual energy and communication. The aura is connected to the spiritual realms and can act as a bridge between the physical world and the higher planes of existence. Through practices like meditation, prayer, or energy healing, individuals can open and activate their aura to receive divine guidance, healing, and inspiration.

How an Aura Is Connected to the Soul

The soul is often described as the essence of a person. It is the part that transcends the physical body and exists beyond the limits of time and space. In contrast, the aura is the energetic counterpart of the physical body and is closely connected to the soul. The aura is an extension of the soul, reflecting its qualities and characteristics. The colors and patterns of the aura can reveal aspects of a person's spiritual nature, including their level of consciousness, inner strengths and weaknesses, and connection to the divine.

The aura is intimately connected to the chakra system, a series of energy centers along the spine. Each chakra corresponds to a different aspect of the body, mind, and soul and influences the aura's qualities associated with that area. For example, the heart chakra is associated with love, compassion, and connection to others and influences the color and texture of the aura in that area. The crown chakra is associated with spiritual connection, enlightenment, and transcendence and influences the higher layers of the aura.

The Different Layers of the Aura

The aura is often described as having multiple layers with unique characteristics and functions. While different traditions and energy healers use slightly different terminology or descriptions for these layers, there are generally considered the aura's seven main layers.

1. **The Physical Layer:** This layer is closest to the physical body and is primarily associated with physical sensations. It is seen as a band of light surrounding the body, extending about one inch to several feet beyond the skin.
2. **The Emotional Layer:** This layer is associated with emotions and feelings and can be seen as a cloud of color surrounding the body. Depending on a person's emotional state, the layer's colors can change rapidly.
3. **The Mental Layer:** This layer is associated with thoughts, ideas, and beliefs and is seen as a network of lines or patterns of light surrounding the body.
4. **The Astral Layer:** This layer is associated with the astral or spiritual realm and is seen as a mist or fog surrounding the body. It is the bridge between the physical and spiritual realms and often the focus of astral projection or out-of-body experiences.
5. **The Etheric Layer:** This layer is associated with vitality and life force energy and is seen as a web or matrix of light surrounding the body. It is often described as the blueprint for the physical body and influences a person's physical health and well-being.
6. **The Celestial Layer:** This layer is associated with higher consciousness and spiritual connection and is seen as a bright, shimmering light surrounding the body. It is often described as the gateway to the divine and is the focus of many spiritual practices and meditations.
7. **The Ketheric Layer:** This layer is associated with the highest levels of consciousness and spiritual enlightenment and is seen as a brilliant, golden light surrounding the body. It is the source of all spiritual energy and the ultimate goal of many spiritual practices and paths.

Each layer of the aura has unique qualities and functions. However, they are all interconnected and influence one another. Individuals can enhance their spiritual growth and connect more deeply with their innermost selves and the divine by purifying and activating each aural layer.

What Can Damage Your Aura?

The aura is a subtle energy field constantly interacting with the environment and is influenced by numerous factors. While the aura is designed to protect the physical body from external negative energies, several things can damage or weaken the aura, including negative emotions and experiences, exposure to harmful energies, and lack of self-care.

1. Negative Emotions and Experiences

Negative emotions and experiences significantly impact the aura. When a person experiences strong emotions, like fear, anger, or sadness, the aura can become clouded or discolored, reflecting the negative energy generated. Over time, repeated exposure to negative emotions can cause the aura to become weakened or damaged, making it more vulnerable to external negative energies. In addition to negative emotions, negative experiences, such as trauma or abuse, can profoundly affect the aura. Traumatic experiences can leave energetic imprints on the aura, causing persistent emotional and physical symptoms. These imprints can be difficult to clear and could require assistance from an energy healer or therapist.

2. Exposure to Harmful Energies

Exposure to harmful energies can damage the aura. Harmful energies can come from a variety of sources, including electromagnetic radiation from electronic devices, geopathic stress from underground water veins or fault lines, and negative energies from people or environments. Electromagnetic radiation from electronic devices, such as computers, cell phones, and televisions, can disrupt the aura's energy field, causing it to weaken or become imbalanced. Geopathic stress, caused by natural radiation from the earth, can negatively affect the aura.

Negative energies from people or environments can harm the aura. Being around negative people or in negative environments can cause the aura to become clouded or discolored, reflecting the negative energy. Being mindful of the people and environments surrounding you and taking steps to protect your aura is important.

3. Lack of Self-Care

A lack of self-care can also damage the aura. Neglecting your physical, emotional, and spiritual needs can cause the aura to become weakened or imbalanced. This includes not getting enough sleep, not eating a healthy diet, not engaging in regular exercise, or not practicing self-care activities, like meditation or yoga. Neglecting your emotional and spiritual needs can negatively affect the aura. Therefore, addressing emotional or spiritual imbalances you might be experiencing and taking steps to heal and strengthen the energy field is essential. Healing methods can include working with an energy healer or a therapist, engaging in spiritual practices like meditation or prayer, or cultivating positive relationships and environments.

How Do You Know if Your Aura Needs Healing?

The aura is a constantly evolving energy field that can weaken or become damaged over time. Awareness of the signs and symptoms of a damaged aura and cultivating self-awareness and intuition to know when your aura needs healing are vital. Various methods, like energy readings and aura photography, are available to provide additional insight into your aura's state.

Signs and Symptoms of a Damaged Aura

Several signs and symptoms can indicate your aura is damaged or needs healing. These include:

- Feeling emotionally drained or overwhelmed
- Experiencing physical symptoms such as fatigue, headaches, or digestive issues
- Feeling disconnected from your body or surroundings
- Being overly sensitive to other people's emotions or energy
- Feeling anxious, depressed, or moody
- Having difficulty sleeping or experiencing vivid dreams
- Feeling heaviness or pressure around the head or shoulders
- Experiencing being spiritually blocked or stuck

Other factors, like physical illness or stress, could cause these symptoms. However, suppose you experience persistent or unexplained symptoms. In that case, it is worth exploring if your aura contributes to your overall health and well-being.

Self-Awareness and Intuition

Self-awareness and intuition are important tools for assessing your aura's state. You can become more attuned to your energy field and better identify when something feels "off" by practicing self-reflection and mindfulness. Paying attention to your intuition and listening to your inner voice provides valuable insight into your aura's condition and whether it requires healing.

Energy Readings and Aura Photography

Energy readings and aura photography are useful tools for those interested in more objective methods of assessing their aura. Energy readings require working with an energy healer or practitioner to assess your aura using various techniques, like scanning, chakra assessment, or muscle testing. Aura photography uses specialized cameras to capture images of the aura and provide visual insight into the state of your energy field.

Ways to Heal a Damaged Aura

If you have identified that your aura could be damaged or needs healing, several methods are available to help restore balance and vitality to your energy field. These methods include aura-cleansing techniques, energy-healing modalities, lifestyle changes, and self-care practices.

Aura Cleansing Techniques

Aura cleansing techniques remove negative energy and blockages from the aura, allowing it to function optimally. Some popular aura-cleansing techniques include:

- **Smudging**: Smudging involves burning herbs like sage or palo santo to clear negative energy from the aura and physical space.
- **Salt baths**: Soaking in a bath infused with Epsom salts or Himalayan salt can help draw out negative energy and promote relaxation.
- **Crystal healing**: Certain crystals, like clear quartz or amethyst, can absorb negative energy and promote healing in the aura.
- **Reiki**: Reiki is energy healing, where the practitioner channels healing energy into the recipient to balance and clear the aura.

- **Sound healing:** Sound healing uses specific frequencies and vibrations, like singing bowls or tuning forks, to promote aura healing.
- **Herbal Baths:** Soaking in a bath infused with herbs like lavender or chamomile can promote relaxation and release negative energy from the aura. Different herbs have different properties that can specifically affect the aura.
- **Flower Essences:** Flower essences are dilutions of flower extracts with energetic properties affecting the aura. These essences can be taken orally or applied topically to promote healing and balance in the aura.

Energy Healing Modalities

Energy healing modalities promote healing and balance in the body's energy systems, including the aura. Some popular energy healing modalities include:

- **Acupuncture:** Acupuncture is inserting thin needles into specific points on the body to promote balance and healing in the energy field.
- **Reflexology:** Reflexology is the application of pressure to specific points on the feet, hands, and ears to promote healing and balance in the energy field.
- **Chakra healing:** Chakra healing works with the body's energy centers (chakras) to promote balance and healing in the aura.
- **Qigong:** Qigong is a Chinese practice using slow, gentle movements, breathing techniques, and meditation to promote balance and healing in the energy field.
- **Pranic Healing:** Pranic healing uses the body's energy centers to remove blockages and promote balance and healing in the energy field.
- **Polarity Therapy:** Polarity therapy balances the body's energy field through touch, movement, and communication techniques. This modality is based on the idea that thoughts, emotions, and physical experiences affect the body's energy field.

- **Access Consciousness:** This method uses various tools and techniques, including verbal processes, bodywork, and energetic clearing, to help individuals access their inner wisdom and create positive life changes. Among the most well-known tools are "The Bars," which touch specific points on the head to release energy blockages and promote relaxation.

Lifestyle Changes and Self-Care Practices

Lifestyle changes and self-care practices are making conscious choices to support the health and well-being of your energy field. Some of the most effective practices include:

- **Meditation:** Meditation is sitting quietly and focusing on your breath or a specific object to promote relaxation and balance in the energy field. Regular meditation can help reduce stress and promote overall well-being.
- **Exercise:** Exercise is an important part of maintaining a healthy energy field. Physical activity can help reduce stress, increase circulation, and promote overall well-being.
- **Healthy diet:** Eating a balanced and nutritious diet can help support your energy field's health by providing essential nutrients and promoting overall well-being.
- **Positive affirmations:** Positive affirmations are repeating positive statements to yourself to promote positive self-talk and emotional well-being.
- **Setting boundaries:** Setting boundaries is establishing clear limits with yourself and others to protect your energy and promote well-being.

Maintaining a Strong Aura

Maintaining a strong aura is essential for overall health and well-being. As you care for your physical body through exercise, healthy eating, and rest, you must care for your energy field to promote optimal health. Here are some creative and effective ways to keep your aura strong and vibrant:

- **Shielding:** Shielding is visualizing a protective shield around your energy field to keep negative energy out and protect your aura. You can imagine the shield as a bubble or a force field surrounding and protecting your energy field.

- **Grounding**: Grounding is connecting with the earth to promote balance and stability in your energy field. Visualize roots growing from your feet into the earth or spend time in nature, like walking barefoot on the ground.
- **Visualizations**: Visualizations use your imagination to create a positive, protective image in your mind. For example, visualize yourself surrounded by a white light protecting your energy field or surrounded by a group of supportive, positive people.
- **Color therapy**: Color therapy uses specific colors to promote balance and healing in the energy field. For example, wearing or surrounding yourself with the color green can promote balance and harmony, while blue can promote calm and communication.
- **Feng shui**: Creating a harmonious and balanced living space through feng shui can help promote a strong aura. It involves arranging your space to promote good energy flow and balance.

By incorporating these effective techniques into your daily routine, you can maintain a strong and healthy aura to support your physical, emotional, and spiritual well-being.

Various methods for healing and maintaining your aura have been provided. Many more are available from online sources or in health stores.

Healing your aura is an essential part of maintaining overall well-being and strengthening psychic protection. By understanding what an aura is, what can damage it, and how to heal it, you can control your energetic state and enhance your spiritual growth. Incorporating regular aura maintenance practices and protection techniques can help you maintain a strong aura and navigate the world with greater ease and confidence.

Chapter 6: Calling Upon Angels for Protection

Angelic beings have assisted humans for thousands of years and are more than willing to guide and help when facing an obstacle or difficult situation. This chapter explains how angels or archangels can protect you, your space, and your loved ones against psychic attacks. You'll learn that angels are beings blessed with immense powers. They can be summoned to work on your behalf, guide you through life, and envelop you with protective energies. They are spiritual creatures in many forms. However, they aren't bound to a physical presence, so they won't appear in their natural form. Angels have different purposes and jurisdictions. For example, archangels have the specialty they govern and can be summoned to resolve specific issues. They are leaders among angels and have an immense energy signature. While people are generally more sensitive to their guardian angel's energy, you can feel an energy shift in the room when an archangel appears. Guardian angels guide you through life from birth, pointing out paths and purposes and helping you heal from past traumas. They rush in to help when you need help or direct your messages to your guardian or archangels.

Guardian angels guide you throughout your life.
https://unsplash.com/photos/Oo9IunFNKcE?utm_source=unsplash&utm_medium=referral&utm_content=creditShareLink

Guardian angels are responsible for your spiritual growth and protect you on your life's journey. Unlike archangels, which work with everyone, guardians work exclusively with their charge. Your guardian angel has a unique bond with you and provides unconditional love and support - and everything else you may need to raise your psychic defenses. While they won't interfere with your conscious decisions, they can be called upon, which is great if you need an urgent power boost to ward off negative vibes.

You can call on an angel when you struggle to keep out negative energies or fear incoming psychic attacks. However, your guardian angel is the closest to you and can absorb your emotions and vibes, so they will know you need them before you actually do. You'll feel your guardian's presence in times of despair or stress caused by negative spiritual influences. They may send you a subtle message to get your attention and help you embrace their protective powers.

Guardian angels aren't only for challenging times. You can call on them whenever you need support and psychic protection. They can help you sustain your energy and guard you as you step into uncharted territories, like meeting people you don't know (hence you are unaware of their intentions and emotions).

While angels (particularly your guardians) are keen to accept your invitation into your life, connecting with them is a highly personal process. You can invoke them as you wish. You can summon one angel or more, as sometimes psychic protection requires several layers of angelic powers.

Calling on Angels for Protection

A simple and sincere prayer is the easiest way to call on an angel. For example, you can say.

"Thank you, (the angel's name you want to summon), for guiding me through this situation. I welcome your guidance and protection."

When summoning an angel for protection, remember their spirit guides you with the highest truth. They carry incredibly high vibrations, regardless of which angel you summon. They deserve your gratitude, so it's always a great idea to begin by addressing them with a "thank you." It also reminds you that angelic help is already on its way.

When first contacting your guardian, spirit guide, or another angel, you must first introduce yourself. While they might know who you are spiritually, it doesn't hurt to be polite and respectful. Summon your guardian angel through a simple mediation.

Instructions:

1. Get comfortable in a secluded space, close your eyes, and take a few long, deep breaths.
2. Using your mind, call on your guardian angel, welcome them, and ask them to reveal their name to you.
3. Use your preferred relaxation method. Use whatever technique helps you become centered, grounded, and focused on a specific intention.
4. You can meditate for as long as you like. You may hear your guardian's name as a thought or an audible sound during meditation. Or they may guide you to write it in your journal.
5. If you don't get a message from your guardian angel in your first meditation, don't worry. You may not be ready to receive it yet, but it is coming. It will probably come through unexpectedly, like in a song or on a license plate.

There are other ways to interact, work with angels, and use their protective powers. Below are a few.

Get to Know the Angel

The first step toward harnessing an angel's energy is by getting to know them. Here is how to learn more about the angel you're working with:

1. Find a quiet space (preferably with a door you can close to shut out other people's energetic influences).
2. Sit comfortably, close your eyes, relax your mind, and get in touch with your intuition. Ask your intuition for the name of angels to help you with your current endeavors.
3. The angel's name will appear in your mind. If it doesn't, the angels are letting you choose who you want to work with. You may even name the angel yourself.
4. If you're invited to name an angel, choose a name that makes you feel protected and loved when you think of them. Their name should make you feel warm and peaceful and smile.
5. Write down the name of the angel you've summoned, so you can call them when needed.
6. Once you have their name, address the angel, ask how they can help you, how they will send you signals, and how you will know they'll protect you. Offer clues on how you want to be protected and contacted, too.
7. Using the angels' names will help you stay more connected to them and make them seem more real and available when you need protection.

Ask Them to Send You a Sign

Angels love sending messages to improve your life or remind you of their loving presence and protection. You can ask them to send you a sign of their protective energies by penning down this request in your journal, expressing it through prayer, asking for it in a spell or ritual, or meditating on your request. After asking for a sign of their protection, you must pay attention to your environment. Look for signs from the angels that you're no longer at risk of physical attacks. They could come in a prophetic dream, a fresh perspective on a problematic situation, or an unexpected opportunity or relationship.

Dedicating Something to Them

Feel free to dedicate songs, poems, or letters to angels. It doesn't matter who the author is. It could be the song you've heard on the radio or a poem you've recently read. All that matters is that the angel understands how you wish to communicate. Once they learn this, they will reassure you of their protection through these means. You could write them a letter or poem. This could be about wanting protection or healing, or expressing gratitude for angelic protection.

Prayer for Angelic Protection

The following prayer is a great tool to evoke your guardian angels. It's an excellent way to honor them and shows you're aware of their presence and will summon them if needed. Your guardian angel will help you ward off malicious affiliations threatening your spiritual well-being.

Instructions:

1. Go to your sacred space and light a candle for the guardian angel.
2. Take a deep breath to center yourself and eliminate distracting thoughts from your mind.
3. Focus on your intention of bringing angelic protection into your life, space, or that of your loved ones.
4. When you're ready, recite the following prayer:

   "My angel, my loving guardian,

   Defend (insert the name) in upcoming challenges,

   So, the good vibes won't be lost when facing negative influences.

   My guardian, you've been by my side throughout my life.

   May you guard me on all my journeys."

Psychic Protection with Archangels

This meditation opens the gate for effective energy cleansing to counteract psychic attacks and remove the remnants of toxic energies from your life. Through it, you can experience the shielding energy of Archangels, the most powerful spiritual protectors in the universe. For example, you can use it to summon Archangel Michael to eradicate all forms of fear and negativity from your life. Whichever archangel you choose to call on, this meditation will help you experience their empowering, guiding presence as they uplift your energies, enabling you to obtain spiritual health and well-being.

Instructions:
1. Find a comfortable place where you won't be disturbed for at least 30 minutes.
2. Close your eyes and deepen your breath to center your mind and ground yourself.
3. When relaxed, visualize your core desires (intent) like a bright sphere glowing with white light.
4. Focus on the sphere and enjoy the silence and peace it brings to your mind. Breathe in - as if trying to pull the calm deep into your body.
5. As you exhale deeply, let go of all other thoughts from your consciousness. Will the calming energy to flow inward, and don't let new thoughts intrude on your consciousness.
6. Allow your intent to transcend the space and imagine it has taken the form of a spacious temple. Visualize yourself stepping into the temple and observing how it looks, feels, and sounds.
7. The temple is your sacred space, where divine energies protect you. No other energy can enter without permission or draw yours out against your will. Here, you have all the power to protect yourself.
8. As you're exploring the temple, feel how the power from the temple radiates throughout your body. You feel security, calmness, love, and well-being.
9. Now, imagine your divine space transforming into an orb of spinning white light. Feel the orb vibrating and floating upward, taking you through space to the luminous horizon above you.
10. As you pass a luminous golden mass traveling toward a source of bright light, you feel enveloped with more love, protection, peace, and joy as energy particles uplift your energies.

11. Feel how the protective energies enter your body, humming like your heartbeat. If you feel guided toward certain thoughts and emotions, feel free to join and follow them.
12. For a moment, return to yourself, and let the newfound emotions wash over you. Return to your previous vision on your next inhale. See the archangel in front of you with his sacred sword by his side.
13. Imagine embracing the angel. They may ask you permission to empower you with protective energy. After granting permission, invite the archangel in, and let them scan your mind, body, and soul to see where you need the most protection.
14. They will identify and source negative energies; with their sword, they will cut through them, detaching them from your body and freeing you from their bonds. They will help you to eliminate the psychic attack remains and reassure you that from now on, one can manipulate your energy without your permission.
15. Breathe deeply and let the negative energies go, assimilating the changes as your energy is cleansed. Notice thoughts and feelings passing through you as the negative influences make their way out of your life.
16. Ask yourself questions related to these emotions. For example, ask yourself who you need to forgive if you feel resentment. To whoever comes to mind, grant forgiveness and replace it with love. If you fear someone negatively impacts your vibes, tell them they no longer have permission to access your energy. Release negative interaction you've engaged in with this person.
17. Slowly let the images go and feel the relief washing over you, intertwined in the waves of forgiveness. The archangel is empowering you with their protective energy. If you need additional help with spiritual healing, ask the archangel to bless you with healing energy.
18. Visualize yourself being enveloped with a white robe, held together with a purple chain - the symbol of the angel's protective powers.

19. The angel creates three glowing orbs of energy around you, each spinning in a different direction. They're connected to your energy; between them is a powerful energy field. Their directions can never be aligned, so no outside force can breach the field.
20. The orbs will watch over you and stand guard to ward off future attacks. They represent a connection to the archangel, who you can now call on more easily.
21. Return to your body and feel re-empowered by your reinforced psychic protection. With a centering breath, open your eyes and return to your life.

Angelic Sigil Magic

Sigils are images of symbols incorporated into different magical acts. They represent the goal or intention you want to manifest - angelic protection. As they are magical tools, sigils must be activated with a ritual. You can use premade angelic sigils or create your own by focusing on what you want to achieve with them and channeling your spiritual energy into that purpose. The energy of the angel to whom the symbol belongs maintains this energy.

Using Angelic Sigils

You must use the correct ritual to establish the line of communication when using angel-summoning sigils. You must choose the right angel for your intention, their association (days, candles, prayers), and the appropriate intention.

Here is a simple summoning spell for angelic protection:

1. On your sacred place, arrange your tools - an angelic sigil, a candle associated with the angel, and another candle to represent your intention (use one candle if your intent matches the angel's powers).
2. Light the candles(s) and take the paper with the charged sigil in your hands.
3. Holding the sigil close to your body, get into a comfortable position and relax, taking a few deep breaths.
4. Close your eyes and visualize the sigil in front of you. If you struggle with this step, you can keep your eyes open and deeply gaze at the sigil.

5. Once your focus is fully on the sigil and other thoughts are eliminated from your mind, state your intention out loud:

"By the power of the angel whose energy is in this sigil,

I ask for my wishes to be granted.

May I and those around me be protected,

And guide on the sacred path of angels."

6. After another deep breath, release the sigil's image and open your eyes (or put the paper with the sigil down) and return to your day-to-day activities.

If the angel you've called on through the sigil wants to send a message, they will do so soon. You may receive this message in your dreams by tapping into your intuition, realizing your intention, reading a book, or in situations or visions related to your angelic sigil spell.

You can summon the power of an angel through sigil magic. However, working with archangels is recommended if you need reinforcement in a specific field (like psychic protection from powerful negative energies). You can invoke them on the days associated with their favorite colors. For example, the Archangel Samuel is best summoned with a rose-colored candle on a Tuesday.

To summon your guardian angel, you'll need the day of the week they've been assigned to you - the day you were born. It is the best way to form a connection to your spiritual guide and use them to make things work in your favor.

Depending on the issue you're dealing with, you can summon the angel best representing your problem (and its solutions) according to their qualities and powers. For example, the Archangel Samuel governs spiritual elevation, protection, and peace, whereas if you need empowerment, faith, and courage to fend off negative energies, you'll need the powers of Archangel Michael.

Chapter 7: Stones, Plants, and Symbols of Protection

As the title implies, this chapter is dedicated to protective crystals, protective plants, and symbols of protection. It lists the most common and potent crystals, plants, and protection symbols, with their spiritual purpose and suggestions for using them for protection purposes. You'll learn to create and charge your sigils of protection.

Protective Crystals

Crystals can help keep you connected to your mind, body, and soul.
https://unsplash.com/photos/bGxyxfqeq34?utm_source=unsplash&utm_medium=referral&utm_content=creditShareLink

Using crystals is a wonderful way of keeping connected to your mind, body, soul, and psychic energies. Using true crystals is recommended, as these were formed from natural ingredients and are a great way to incorporate nature into your daily life. Crystals vibrate at different frequencies. For example, the vibes of some stones can help you fend off psychic attacks. Others will help you flush out energy that is not serving you.

While certain crystals are better for psychic protection than others, the best stones are those you're drawn to. The crystal's energy will feel inviting to you, connecting with your energy. It can make you pause, learn to raise your vibrations, and protect yourself. Below are a few crystals with pronounced protective energies.

Black Tourmaline

Black tourmaline can be an incredibly potent protector for your aura. Its energy has grounding and soothing effects. Its energy provides calming and anchoring qualities. It can stop harmful energy that someone else is sending your way. Negative thinking patterns, often associated with psychic attacks, can be banished by the healing energies of this black stone. For instance, unfavorable influences can make you experience severe anxiety. Black tourmaline has the power to calm your mind, push away worry-filled thoughts, and give you the confidence you once had. Black tourmaline is one of the best crystals to add to your collection if you want to block out all the negative energy from your life, your environment, and the lives of others around you.

The best way to use black tourmaline for protection is during meditation. While holding the stone, you only need to consider what you wish to be protected from. Alternatively, you can wear black tourmaline if you struggle with persistently pessimistic thoughts, anxiety, or dread of harmful energy or keep it in your pocket. It creates a protective energy bubble around you.

Obsidian

The second black gemstone on this list, obsidian, absorbs negative energy like the color black incorporates all other colors. When you are afflicted by negative energy, this crystal can help you to overcome those moments. When you are experiencing negative vibrations that are weighing you down with heavy thoughts, it can help you to find clarity. Uncomfortable truths about your emotions and interpersonal connections may come to light. It can help you identify anything another person is trying to conceal from you.

Since it absorbs all negative energy around you, obsidian is not a stone you can always wear, and it must be cleansed often. However, you can place it around your home. Setting this stone by entryways blocks negative energy threatening to enter your space, halting it in its tracks. By absorbing these negative energy vibrations and returning them as positive ones, obsidian will shield your home and everyone inside from that negative energy.

Amethyst

Amethyst can help with psychic shielding while being mostly recognized for relieving stomach aches and other stress-related ailments. This purple stone promotes tranquil, calming energy and protects against overpowering feelings that cause anxiety and despair. Amethyst provides emotional and spiritual protection by stabilizing mental health. It helps you become more conscious of bad energy and the necessity to eliminate it from your life.

Amethyst can be put to many different uses. You can keep it near where you frequently are, wear it as a charm on a bracelet or necklace, or keep it in your pocket. Placing the stone under your pillow as you sleep will provide additional protection for dream work and spiritual contact, even when your conscious mind is asleep.

Clear Quartz

Due to its innate ability to connect with other natural energies, clear quartz can take on the energy of other crystals near it. You can use clear quartz to amplify the energy of a protective crystal you're using. Besides manifesting more protection in your life, this stone can be used for purification. Clear quartz cleanses energy and empowers your natural protective abilities by flushing out negative vibes from your mind, body, and soul.

If you want to use it as a cleansing stone, wear clear quartz as a charm or put it in your pocket. If you want to amplify the potency of other crystals, use them alongside in rituals and spells. For example, you can move it up and down in front of your body or hold it close to your heart and over another crystal while casting a protection spell. It will shield your energy and release negative vibes from the body.

Pyrite

Pyrite is a golden crystal guarding your energy against negative vibes. If you have been to a crystal shop, you have probably seen this beauty.

Its golden color manifests abundance and boosts confidence, which is handy when increasing your psychic protection. This stone helps you release negativity and manifest positive changes in your life by making you more confident about protecting yourself from outside influences.

Pyrite is incredibly powerful and can be effective regardless of how you use it. Whether you want to keep it in your bag or pocket or put it in the entryways of your home or office - it will protect you. If you want to wear it or keep it close to your body, you must cleanse it often with clear quartz so it can shield you wherever you go.

Smithsonite

Smithsonite is not only beautiful, but it's also the stone with the most serene energy. Its vibrations can help calm the emotions caused by negative vibes emanating from other people. It can center you, helping you relax and focus on erecting the necessary protection against harmful influences.

Smithsonite is best used for protecting your home or office space. Place it in a special place (like an altar or other sacred area) to help you ward off unhealthy energies from your home. Or keep it in your drawer at the office, reminding you of its protective powers on a stressful day with toxic coworkers.

Black Jade

Another black stone on the list is black jade. It can help you connect with your intuition and learn which people to avoid. Your intuition knows who emanates negative vibes or in which situations you are most likely to be affected. Black jade will help you identify where negativity enters your life and eliminate the root of your energy issues.

You can use black jade as a personal (energy) guardian and take it with you wherever you go, wearing it as a charm or keeping it in your pocket. It will be particularly effective when you meet new people, travel to new places, or venture into new experiences.

Protective Plants

Like natural stones, plants are connected to nature and its universal power that provides healing and connects all living beings. You use natural energy to protect yourself from physical attacks and cleanse your energy. Due to this, placing plants in certain areas of your home or workspace has plenty of benefits on your vibrations. Looking at greenery reduces stress, improves mood, and eliminates other symptoms of toxic energetic influences. Plants enable you to defend yourself against bad energies by improving your physical and mental health. Plants give out positive energy and eliminate toxic energies from their surroundings.

Moreover, plants produce immense amounts of oxygen, which is good for the environment. All living beings that thrive on oxygen will be filled with more positive energy, including people. The more positive vibes in the environment, the more sources you'll have to tap into when you need an added boost of good vibes to fend off toxic influences. Here are plants for spiritual protection:

Basil

The deep green leaves of basil emanate plenty of positive energy. They have antioxidant properties, which improve the metabolism of all beings laced with positive energy. It increases the positive energy in your environment and is a powerful aid in spiritual protection.

You can use basil in many ways for psychic protection. For example, you can use them to anoint candles for protective spells and rituals. Put dried basil in a satchel (with other protective herbs) and place it under your pillow. Or, you can keep a pot of basil plant on a windowsill to block out negative energies from your home.

Aloe Vera

The aloe vera plant is of the most common houseplants for psychic protection, albeit its use is often unintentional. Many people know of this plant's healing, soothing, and stress-relieving properties. However, these can also protect your aura.

Since aloe vera can survive any weather, you can keep it anywhere in your home or workplace. Placing the plant near where you spend most time will fill you with plenty of positive vibes and flush out negative energy. Take advantage of its healing and cleansing properties by creating homemade lotions for added protection.

Sage

The sage plant is another herb to help you eliminate toxic energy from your surroundings. It enables you to flush out negative emotions (including anger and fear) caused by bad vibes.

Plant sage in small pots, and place them in your home where you need the most protection. You can use dried sage for cleansing rituals like ritual baths or smudging. The former is great for flushing out negative influences from your body, while the latter eliminates them from your surroundings. Or, you can use the dried herb as anointment in protective rituals and ceremonies, place it under your pillow in a satchel, or keep it with you as a talisman.

Vetiver

Vetiver is another houseplant linked to improving mental health; it elevates spiritual protection. Vetiver encourages positive energy flow and helps reduce toxic energy flow. Its calming aurora helps relax your mind and improves sleep, enhancing your ability to ward off negative influences. You can place vetiver anywhere you need the most protection.

Lavender

Lavender's soothing aroma helps reduce stress, boosts relaxation, and flushes out toxic energies from your body. Besides relieving symptoms of stress and depression, lavender is also great for spiritual protection. Its oils eliminate negative vibes from the environment and encourage the flow of positive energies.

Lavender can be used in oil, fresh, or dried. For example, use dried lavender in a spiritual cleansing bath or smudging. Lavender oil and fresh flowers can be used in purification rituals, contributing to the accumulation of positive energy to protect you from toxic vibes.

Jasmine

Jasmine can bring positive energy into romantic or close familial relationships. Place this plant anywhere around your house to surround everyone with good vibes. It is particularly effective if you believe someone is trying to cause a rift in your relationship with their negative vibes.

Thyme

Thyme is another aromatic herb known to boost vibes. It can bring you good luck and confidence in your abilities. Like sage, you can use dry thyme in rites and spells to fight off negative energy. Or, incorporate it into cleansing rituals, like baths and smudging. Dried or fresh thyme near your bed (including under your pillow) helps improve sleep and spiritual communication through sleep and wards off nightmares.

Peace Lily

The peace lily boosts positive energy flow around your home or office space, helping protect yourself from negative influences in your private and professional life. The plant purifies the air, effectively reducing headaches and other symptoms of stress caused by toxic energies. Place it anywhere with little sunlight. It will charge itself and your surroundings with even more protective energy.

Jade Plant

Like the peace lily, the jade plant helps improve your mood by eliminating negative energies from your environment. It gives you more confidence to defend yourself and your loved ones from psychic attacks. Keep the jade plant at the home's entrance, and all those inside it will be protected.

Symbols of Protection

Symbols have been used for spiritual protection since ancient times. All cultures employ some symbolism during protective spells and rituals. Below are a few of the most powerful symbols of psychic protection.

Triquetra

The triquetra, known as the trinity knot, is one of the oldest protective symbols. It consists of three interlaced arcs, with loops knotted together, forming a triangle. The triquetra has been used in pagan cultures and Celtic fold magic, but its uses have been traced to Asian regions. In Celtic mythology, the triquetra denotes the three natural realms - the sky, the sea, and the earth.

The symbol can represent your body's physical, mental, and spiritual states. Hence, it's great for overall spiritual protection. You can wear the triquetra as a charm or keep it close to your body to protect you on the go. Or, incorporate it into rituals and spells when you need added reinforcement to ward off toxic influences.

Turtle

Due to their long lifespan, turtles are lucky charms in many cultures. The animal has hard body armor, which symbolizes spiritual strength and resilience. The turtle signifies a power for protection against harmful energies. It reminds you that you can overcome any obstacle as long as you can ward off toxic vibes. Even if your goal might seem far away, by slowly building your spiritual energies, you'll reach it. No matter how many hurdles you face, a turtle symbol will help you stay motivated and determined to reach your goals. The best way to use this symbol for psychic protection is to wear it as an amulet.

Helm of Awe

This protection symbol comes from Norse mythology, associated with protection against enemies. Viking tribes painted this symbol on their bodies before battle to invite good luck and protection. Besides offering protection against toxic energies, the helm of awe is used to dissipate fears. It's depicted as eight tridents centered on a core area, shielding it from evil. It's a reminder that no matter how potent the negative energy is, you will always be protected by it. This symbol helps suppress your fears, giving you confidence in your choices and abilities to defend your aura from negative influences. You can incorporate it into protective rituals and spells, or wear it as a charm or talisman for an added protection layer when heading onto uncharted territories, like meeting new people and situations.

The Evil Eye

The evil eye is another commonly used and revered protection symbol used globally. Known as *nazar*, the evil eye symbol is associated with inner sight. It improves self-awareness and draws attention to areas that need protection. The symbol is depicted as a blue-and-white picture of an eye.

The symbol can repel negative energies, especially if worn as jewelry, charm, or talisman. It protects you from harmful influences, including those emanating from people wishing you bad luck and misfortune. It replies to jealous thoughts and any associated bad vibes. Incorporate it into your decor and furniture to protect your home.

Dragonfly

The dragonfly is known for its transformative abilities. It's a powerful symbol of self-actualization and spiritual elevation. With spiritual advancement comes a higher ability to ward off negative vibes.

Dragonflies are connected to fire and water energy, the duality reminding you of the balance of the opposing aspects in your life. They are associated with new beginnings and goals in your personal and professional life.

Using a dragonfly symbol for spiritual protection can help you invite more positive energy into your life, replacing negativity. It can inspire you to look at the bright side of every situation (no matter how challenging) rather than being consumed by negative influences.

Wear the symbol as a charm or talisman daily to brighten up your life and become more confident in protecting your spiritual energies. It will help you prosper in your spiritual journey, adding light and happiness to your life.

How to Create and Charge Symbols

You can create your own signs (sigils) for protection. All you need is a sheet of paper, a pencil, and a candle (in color representing your intention) to make your sigils.

Instructions:
1. Write the reason for your sigil on the paper. For example, you can pen down your need for protection from a spiritual guide. Write it as something you've already achieved rather than something you wish to achieve.
2. Cross out all the vowels and consonants appearing more than once in your writing. Create a sentence with the remaining letters. Then, create a symbol incorporating each word's first letter.
3. Activate the sigil by writing it on another piece of paper while focusing on your intention. Put the sigil aside; don't think about it until you need it. Alternatively, you can burn the paper with the sigil on it.
4. You can use the sigil to summon protective energy. For example, if you're calling on a protective power of an angel, the sigil will help get in touch with the angel to whom the symbol belongs and maintain this energy.

After activating the sigil, you must charge your symbol to empower it with protective energy. You can do this by:
- Storing it somewhere meaningful
- Carving it into a candle and lighting it
- Drawing a protective sigil on your body
- Tracing a sigil in the air and visualizing its dissipation
- Drawing a sigil into your food and eating it

Chapter 8: Breaking Curses, Hexes, and Attachments

This chapter enlists several spells and rituals to defend against curses, hexes, and unwanted attachments and relationships. It explains curses and hexes, their differences, why they happen, and how to identify if you are a victim of one.

Curses and Hexes

Curses and hexes are spells that can bring harm to a target.
https://unsplash.com/photos/x69K221AGHw?utm_source=unsplash&utm_medium=referral&utm_content=creditShareLink

Hexes are simple negativity-inducing spells cast by a person with evil intent. Depending on how they are cast, hex spells can be more formal than curses. Sometimes they require a handy spell, while at other times, they need a complicated ritual. It depends on how much the person wishes to harm their target. However, even the most evil-intentioned and potent hexes can be broken.

A curse is also a spell that hurts its target by bringing bad luck, misfortune, illness, financial hardship, and other hurdles into their life. There are two primary curses: The chaos curse, which leads to random negative events, and the entropy curse, which targets a person or several people and increases the likelihood of being afflicted by negative vibes. Curses can be personal or generational.

The number of different curses and hexes used by witches is vast, but a few common ones are used to impart the same sentiments. For example, the evil eye is caused by envy, hatred, jealousy, malice, anger, and resentment. Although there are several evil eyes, they all have one thing in common - they are born from a magic spell cast by someone who wants to harm you.

How to Identify if You're a Victim of a Curse or Hex

Curses and hexes are more common than you may realize. Here are tips on how to recognize if you're a victim of a curse or hex:

1. The feeling of defeat, discouragement, and depression: You feel completing even the simplest task seems hopeless and overwhelming, and you're constantly disappointed in yourself or feel like giving up on everything.
2. You're plagued by physical fatigue, constantly get sick, or generally feel a lack of energy or motivation.
3. You lack a desire for spiritual development: You may have difficulty praying, connecting to spiritual guides, or performing practices for spiritual enlightenment.
4. Loss of faith: You may feel let down by your spirit guides – and they're now punishing you.
5. A negative view on life: You could be wrestling with anxious thoughts, worries, or fears or feel nobody cares for you.
6. Consider returning to old practices regardless of how harmful they were to your spiritual health. Curses can cause you to consider moving backward instead of forward with your life.

7. Reopening old emotional wounds: Even if you believe you've closed a painful chapter of your life, a curse or hex can reopen them, making you deal with the hurt all over again.
8. Feeling guilt, shame, and condemnation constantly: You may feel your thoughts, emotions, and actions are not good enough for you to be accepted.
9. Feeling rejected, lonely, and thinking you don't belong: You feel no one understands your feelings, so you cannot belong anywhere.
10. Confusion over belief and ideas: Psychic attacks can cause you to doubt your beliefs and question your reality.

Curse or Hex Removal with Lemon and Sea Salt

This simple curse or hex removal ritual uses salt's spiritual cleansing properties and lemon's revitalizing energy. It banishes negativity from inside and around your body. Don't use it if you have open wounds or cuts.

Ingredients:

- A lemon
- Sea salt

Instructions:

1. Cut your lemon in half, and cover each half with sea salt.
2. Wipe the lemons over your body, one half at a time. Cleanse your aura and channel the toxic energy brought on by a curse or hex into the lemon.
3. Throw away the lemon when you have finished. Otherwise, the bad energy continues lingering around you.
4. You should feel better a few hours after the ritual. However, it's best to repeat it for at least a week. You can do it as long as you feel the toxic energies and other effects of curses around you.

Salt Water Bath to Break a Hex

Magical baths are spells for breaking curses and hexes. It's an excellent spiritual cleansing. It helps break off the negative energy flow directed toward you and replenishes its void with plenty of positive vibes. For the best effects, perform this ritual at night, during the waning moon phase. The latter is associated with banishing, withdrawing, and eliminating negative things from a person's life or space. The sea (and, by extension, sea salt) is associated with the moon, so this ritual creates a powerful link between a banishing bath and lunar magick.

Ingredients:

- 1 cup of sea salt
- 1 cup of Epsom salts
- A glass of water
- 1/4 cup of baking soda

Instructions:

1. Draw water into your bathtub and add the baking soda and salts to the bathwater. Place the glass of water on the tub's rim.
2. Stir the water counterclockwise to combine the ingredients.
3. Before getting into the bath, hold your hands in a prayer position and close your eyes.
4. Visualize the water being filled and surrounded with an orb of bright, white light.
5. Get in the tub and soak for at least 30 minutes.
6. While it helps remove negative energy deep within you, soaking in salty water can be very dehydrating. Feel free to sip from the glass of water to stay hydrated.
7. Once you have finished soaking, exit the tub and dry off.
8. Open your window, and ask the waning moon to finish cleansing you of curses and hexes during the night.

Calling On Spiritual Guides to Banish Negative Energy

Banishing curses can be as simple as asking your spiritual guides to boost your psychic protection. Whether you prefer to work with deities, angels, ancestral spirituals, or other guides, praying to them can help you explore negativity in your life. Whether you were cursed or hexed by a person's malicious intent or an evil spirit, your spirit guides, guardian angels, deities, and ancestral spirits won't hesitate to help you. They can help you identify the source of the bad magic, remove it, direct it back to the spell-caster, and bless you with positivity. If the entity can't help you, it will direct your message to a more powerful one. For example, if your guardian angel can't help by removing your curse or protecting you against it, they will advise you to call on an archangel to help you.

Ingredients:

- A candle associated with the deity, angel, or spirit you're summoning
- A representation of the deity, angel, or spirit you're summoning
- A prayer addressed to the deity, angel, or spirit you're summoning

Instructions:

1. Light the candle and assume a relaxed position in front of your altar, shrine, or other sacred space. It helps if this space is dedicated to the being you're summoning.
2. Focusing on your intent, recite the prayer. You can repeat it several times if you wish. Meditate on your intent after you've finished praying.
3. Thank the entity you summoned for their attention and the blessing they'll provide you with in the future.
4. Repeat your prayer the next day. Working the prayer into your everyday life enables you to build a strong bond with the entities you're addressing. The stronger the relationship, and the more dedicated you are to it, the more this entity will help you repeal or break curses and hexes.

A Crystal Wand Ritual for Spiritual Cleansing

Crystal wands are excellent tools for cleansing your body, home, or another space of negative energy curses and hexes. Alternatively, use crystals instead of crystals wands. The rituals also use other crystals to replenish positive energy. Choose the stone that suits your needs best and replaces negativity with positivity in all the right places. For example, after eliminating the curse or hex's energy from your professional space, use stones that bring good luck and fortune. If you've eliminated the person who affected your self-esteem's energy, you'll need crystals that help you nurture self-love.

Ingredients:
- A crystal that absorbs or counteracts negative energy
- A crystal to fill in the space or yourself with positivity

Instructions:
1. Stand by an open window so the negative energy can leave you and your space as soon as possible. Even if you're only cleansing your space, don't forget to open the windows so the bad vibes have somewhere to go. Otherwise, they will just infect your space and you instead of leaving.
2. In one motion, sweep the crystal (or crystal wand) over your body. Then, move the crystal toward the window, directing the toxic energy away from you and out the window. Do this if you want to eliminate negative influences from your person.
3. Start further from the window to remove curses, hexes, or other malicious vibes from a space. Slowly advancing, move your crystal toward the window several times. When you reach the window, move the crystal as if directing the energy outside.
4. Once you've dispelled the negative energies from your person or space, close your window and take a positivity-bringing crystal. If you've cleansed yourself, sweep the crystal over your body, focusing on filling yourself with positivity.
5. If you've cleansed your space, walk around with the second crystal, focusing on the same intention.

Cleansing Ritual to Remove Curses

This cleansing ritual with eggs will help you remove the evil eye and other common curses from your person. It uses the egg as a vessel for the toxic energy caused by the curse. The curse is drawn away from the person and channeled into the egg.

Ingredients:
- An egg
- A candle (optional)
- A jar
- Water

Instructions:
1. Stand in front of your altar or sacred space with the egg in your hands.
2. Calm your mind and focus on your intention. If you work with deities or spiritual guides, call on them to empower and help you put the curse into the egg.
3. Rub the egg over your body, focusing on areas where you feel discomfort or pain, which could indicate the accumulation of negative energies.
4. You may feel chills around parts of your body, and this is a good sign. It means the egg is drawing negativity from you.
5. Then say the following three times:

    "May all the curses leave my body, mind, and soul, now."

6. Once you feel the egg has absorbed all the negative energies, fill the jar with water and crack the egg into it.
7. Try to read the egg to see the source of the curse. Pay attention to the different shapes, like flowers, people, and other characteristics you can discern as the egg mixes with the water.
8. Once you've finished observing the egg-water mixture, flush it down the toilet.

A Magical Poppet to Banish Bad Magic

Using a poppet (a small doll made from cloth, clay, wood, wax, paper, or other material), you can redirect energy from a person or draw it toward them. Besides people, poppets can represent animals and inanimate objects. Sometimes, poets can embody the soul of a person who died and left a curse or hex behind or was cursed or hexed themselves before death. The spell uses the poppet to represent you or your loved ones and redirect toxic energies directed at you or another person.

Ingredients:

- A poppet - you can buy or make one. For example, you can sew a cotton doll and stuff it with items representing the person you want to protect.
- More items representing you or another person you want to protect (pictures, trinkets, or anything else tied to the person's energy)
- A mirror

Instructions:

1. Take the poppet and the other items to the mirror and hold the doll facing the mirror. If the spell is for you, look into the poppets eyes, and say:

   "As I look into this doll's eye, I become at one with it.

   All evil I may receive will go into this doll,

   And I will be spared from toxic energies."

2. If the spell is for someone else, you can have the person with you and have them repeat the above chant. Or, if you're working remotely, say:

   "This doll is now (the person's name).

   May they be protected from evil,

   As their doppelganger absorbs any toxic energies."

3. Leave the doll in a safe place and let it soak up the negative energies (hexes and ill intent) sent your way or the way of the person you want to protect.

4. If you or the other person have experienced signs of being cursed or hexed, these signs will soon go away.

A Candle Ritual to Remove Evil Forces from Your Environment

This candle magic ritual mixes the power of a black and a white candle. The first is associated with evil, death, and darkness. It denotes the absence of light and is often used to represent night, mourning, and grief. The white candle embodies purity, spirituality, innocence, light, goodness, truth, harmony, peace, love, unity, and balance. White is linked to the stars, moon, angels, and soul. Combining these colors, you can absorb negative forces from your space and replace them with positive vibes.

Ingredients:
- A small white candle
- A small black candle

Instructions:
1. Place the white and a black candle in front of you on your altar or other sacred space. Light them.
2. Calm your mind and say a prayer of gratitude for the positivity in your life to reinforce your intent to chase away negativity.
3. Focus on what your wish to eliminate from your space (your home or workplace) and what you want this space to be filled with.
4. Leave the candles to burn down completely. Avoid blowing them out because it could cause your spell to be disrupted. It's best to perform this spell late in the afternoon when you have plenty of time to supervise the candles before going to bed.

Freezing Spell for Unwanted Attachments

Freezing or souring is used to freeze someone out of your life. You can use them on people who cause you energetic blockages or taint your energy with their toxic vibes. These could be your enemies, people who spread gossip about you while pretending to care about you, or anyone envious of your successes. Don't use it on people you wish to reconcile with later and don't cast the spell in anger. Traditionally you would use salt or vinegar for the spell. Salt can help you make a person's hurtful words bitter in their mouth, severing your connection to them. Vinegar will sour the person, so they'll stop attaching their negative vibes to yours.

Ingredients:
- Sealable container (freezer bag, jar, etc.).
- Charged water (salt or vinegar water) – alternatively, use tap water. However, it will make the spell less effective.
- Totem - to represent the person (or situation you encounter this person) to freeze. It could be a photograph of them, their belongings, or their name on a piece of paper.
- Fruit and vegetables.
- Details of the situations written on paper (in case you are detaching yourself from unhealthy situations).
- Black candle wax - for sealing (optional).
- Black pepper or chili flakes (optional, for making the person's lies or gossip burn in their mouth).

Instructions:
1. Prepare the totem and the written details of the situation (if using any) on your altar, shrine, or other sacred space.
2. Light the black candle. Place the totem (and the paper with the details) in the empty container.
3. Put the fruit and vegetables into the container. If you're using chili or pepper flakes, add them.
4. Fill the container with salt or vinegar water. Close the container.
5. Seal the container by dripping black candle wax on the opening or lid. As you do this, meditate on your intention. Imagine your connection to this person being severed and them disappearing from your life. Revere on the feeling of satisfaction this image brings you.
6. Alternatively, wrap the container in aluminum foil. Ensure the foil's shiny side faces inward so the person's negative energy bounces back to them. You could combine both techniques by sealing the container with wax, then wrapping it in foil for added spell potency.
7. Put the container in the freezer. Leave it there for as long as required for the spell to take effect.

8. Once the spell is complete, remove the container from the freezer, toss its contents into the trash, or leave them in a bin near a crossroads. These options are the safest when the person has been successfully frozen out of your life.
9. Alternatively, leave the container in the freezer and forget about it. It signals that you cannot be bothered to toss it out because the person doesn't deserve your energy thinking of them.
10. If the spell hasn't worked or the person has reappeared in your life, don't toss out the spell. You must recharge it instead. Remove the container from the freezer, thaw it for a few days, and return it to the freezer after meditating on your intention.
11. If you're dealing with a particularly strong attachment, repeat the above process every few days to intensify the spell's power. Continue until the person stops contacting you, gossiping about you, or doing anything against you for good.

Hexes and curses can be broken, regardless of the intent's strength. Use your entities' power to help you break free from a spell.

Chapter 9: Shielding Yourself and Your Loved Ones

If only you could always be surrounded by positivity without harmful influences or energies seeping into your life. However, this isn't realistic. There is no escape from the negativity. Psychic attacks can occur anytime and anywhere, either by accident or on purpose. In other words, you can't control where or how you get these attacks, but you can shield yourself and your family from them.

This chapter provides multiple protection rituals, tips, and techniques to keep yourself and your loved ones safe.

Remember, perform preparation and cleansing rituals before you practice any technique.

Rituals can be used to protect yourself and your loved ones from harm.
https://unsplash.com/photos/x5hvhMBjR3M?utm_source=unsplash&utm_medium=referral&utm_content=creditShareLink

Clearing Ceremony

A clearing ceremony is an effective technique against psychic attacks. It involves burning sage, where the smoke releases dark energy from your body and shields you from future negative influences.

Ingredients:

- Sage smudge stick
- Lavender or sandalwood

Instructions:

1. Put the sage and lavender in the same bundle.
2. Light the herbs with a match, blow out the fire, and place them in a large bowl.
3. Set the intention to shield yourself from dark influences and psychic attacks. You can say a prayer, *"I am protecting myself from the dark forces holding power over me."*
4. Sit on the floor and look up to ask the universe to give you strength and wisdom against these dark forces.
5. Look down at the ground beneath you and feel your connection with Mother Earth. Thank her for the blessings she bestows on you and for allowing you to eliminate these attacks.
6. Cleanse yourself with the sage and let the smoke wash away the negativity.
7. Close your eyes and visualize a protective circle surrounding you, keeping you safe.

You can perform this ritual at your office to protect yourself against psychic attacks in the workplace.

Journaling

Not all dreams are messages from your subconscious. You can experience psychic attacks in your sleep as nightmares or night terrors. People are always vulnerable in the dream world since they have no control over their actions or environment.

Many people don't pay attention to their dreams, while others don't remember them, so you may not be aware that you are experiencing these attacks in your sleep. You may wake up feeling exhausted or stressed, but you don't know why, or you remember your nightmare but don't think much about it.

Tracking your dreams can protect you from psychic attacks while you sleep. Keep a journal by your bedside and write down all your dreams and nightmares when you first wake up before you forget them. Write how you felt in these dreams, like fear, sadness, or anger, and if these emotions stay with you after you wake up.

If you struggle with recalling your dreams, every night before you go to sleep, pray to the universe to help you remember them. Seek the protection of your guardian angels or ancestors to keep you safe in the dream world when you are alone and helpless. Ask them to bless you with happy and light dreams, filling you with love and comfort. You could listen to binaural beats while falling asleep, listening to two tones with different frequencies in each ear. This method leads the brain to create the illusion of a third tone which improves your memory and attention and makes you relax.

Before sleeping, repeat this mantra;

"Dear spirit guides, please provide me with guidance and protection in the dream world."

Cut the Cord and Earth Cording

You can regularly perform these effective and simple techniques. Practice Earth cording in the morning and cord cutting at night.

Ingredients: A bowl of salt water

Instructions:
1. Before you sleep, sit in your bed, close your eyes, and visualize a cord coming out of your belly connecting you to someone or thing (it can be the person attacking your energy or an object you believe is causing psychic attacks).
2. Pretend your fingers are scissors and cut the cord between you and the negative energy source impacting your life. If there is more than one person or object behind these attacks, imagine multiple cords coming out of each of your seven chakras connecting you to them, and cut each individually.
3. Repeat this affirmation while cutting the cords:

    "I release energetic attachments to protect myself from negativity and psychic attacks."

4. After cutting the cords, visualize placing them in the saltwater bowl.

Earth Cording Instructions:
1. In the morning, after you wake up, sit on the ground comfortably and close your eyes.
2. Visualize a cord or more coming out of your belly and connecting you to the Earth. The cords are nurturing, flexible, and strong. You are at one with the Earth, which sustains and protects you. Nothing and no one is strong enough to cut these cords or separate you from Mother Earth.

Strengthen Your Aura

Instructions:
1. Stand in a quiet place without distractions, close your eyes, and breathe in and out deeply.
2. Imagine the colors of each of your seven chakras surrounding you like wheels.
3. Imagine the wheels expanding with every breath until they merge, creating a large colorful circle around you and shielding you from external energies.
4. You are in control of your auric field, and nothing can get in or out without your permission.
5. Repeat this mantra during the visualization, *"I only allow positive vibes in and prevent negativity from coming near me."*

Let Light Surround You

Instructions:
1. Sit comfortably and visualize your heart and the space around it as a white flame.
2. Take deep breaths and imagine the flame growing with every breath until it becomes a big circle surrounding and shielding you.
3. The white light is coming out of you and is part of your being. You are protecting yourself, and this makes you

powerful.

4. Repeat this mantra, *"I am guided and protected. I am the light, and nothing can touch me."*

Meditation Technique #1

Instructions:
1. Sit in a quiet room with no distractions.
2. Get comfortable and relax your body and mind.
3. Close your eyes and take a few deep breaths until your mind is clear.
4. Imagine a bubble of golden energy surrounding you.
5. The bubble is transparent and acts as a shield against negative energy.
6. Imagine dark, negative energy coming toward you, but the protective shield prevents it from getting in.
7. Now, visualize positive and loving energy approaching you and filling the golden bubble.
8. Repeat these steps until you feel comfortable and believe you are protected. The golden bubble is filled with positive energy nourishing you and is strong enough to defend against psychic attacks.

Meditation Technique #2

Instructions:
1. Find a quiet space with no distractions.
2. Lie down and close your eyes.
3. Breathe deeply and take a few minutes to enjoy the peace and quiet.
4. Let go of all your expectations, worries, anxieties, and fears.
5. Think positive thoughts, and let them fill you with joy, compassion, and gratitude.
6. Take a deep breath and let out a long sigh.
7. Scan your body to assess your energy.
8. Breathe in positivity and breathe out negativity for a couple of minutes.

9. Pause for a minute.
10. Focus on your crown chakra (the top of your head).
11. Visualize your energy as a bright light shining over the top of your head.
12. Now, the light is surrounding you, and you feel safe.
13. Spend time focusing on the light.
14. It isn't the light protecting you; it merely acts as your boundary, reminding you that you are in control. You will not allow negative entities into your personal space.
15. Imagine the light getting closer and closer to your body until it becomes an extra layer of skin.
16. Think of the energy you want to embrace, like empowerment or nourishment.
17. Pause for a minute.
18. Think of the energy you want to shield yourself from, like negative thoughts, guilt, or shame.
19. Allow yourself to control your energy, as now you know what you will let in and what you will prevent from coming near you.
20. You are now fully aware of your energy and will notice if it changes or is under attack.
21. Your shield is a part of you, so always keep it up. It prevents people from crossing a line and attacking your energy.
22. Practice this meditation every morning.

Visualization

Instructions:
1. Sit in a comfortable position or lie down in a quiet room.
2. Place pink rose quartz around you or hold one in your hand.
3. Take a few deep breaths and remain quiet for a while.
4. Let go of the tension and stress until you feel calm and relaxed.
5. Focus on creating a blue protective shield.

6. Set an intention. Say:

   "I intend to create a protective shield of divine love and light."

7. Imagine a wall of mirrors surrounding you facing outward. So, if you are under a psychic attack, the negative energy will be reflected outward.
8. Your shield is sealed to prevent unwanted energy from getting to you.
9. Set an intention for only love and joy to get through, and you will only send positive vibes out to the universe.
10. You are inside the shield. Imagine the pink rose quartz's energy surrounding and embracing you.
11. Feel the shield around you as if it's giving you a big hug. Stay with it for a while and repeat your intention.

Steer Clear from Negative People

If you know the people who attack your energy, avoid them as much as possible. All these methods are powerful enough to protect you. However, like any shield, it can weaken with constant exposure to negativity. If you feel your aura or energy altering around certain people, limit your interactions with them. Cut them off if possible, or spend less time with them. However, if this is someone you have to interact with daily, like a family member or your boss, keep your shield up and wear a protective gemstone or symbol whenever you are around them. Place a protective crystal or plant on your desk if this is someone you work with.

Chanting

Chanting is another powerful defense against psychic attacks. Create a chant reflecting your desire for the universe to protect you, write it on your phone, and read it a few times during the day. If you can't think of a chant, use this one or something similar.

"Spirits of the ancestors, guardian angels, and divine universe,

I am grateful for the cleansing white light you have bestowed upon me, healing me from all the darkness and negativity. I ask for your help and guidance to release everything that is not serving me and bringing me harm. Please protect my aura and space and only allow loving light and energy to flow through me. I pray you will send me healing energy to shield me. Thank you for all your blessings."

Affirmations
- I am protected by a white light.
- I only attract positive energy, and negativity has no power over me.
- Positive thoughts and energy constantly surround me.
- My protective shield prevents negative thoughts from coming my way.
- I am filled with light healing me from negativity.
- I am surrounded by happiness and won't allow negative vibes into my space.
- I am a force of light and love; nothing can touch me.
- I am connected to Mother Earth; she protects me from dark energies.
- I release negative energy to Mother Earth and only embrace positive vibes.
- I am strong. Psychic attacks don't bother me.
- I am a walking shield, and negative energy can't reach me.
- My body is filled with positivity; there is no space for dark energies.
- My shield is powerful. Nothing and no one can get through.
- I am in control of my auric field and will not allow anyone or anything to alter my aura.
- I am surrounded by a powerful protective field.
- I will not allow (name person) negative influences to get to me.
- (Name person) has no power over me.
- (Name person) isn't allowed in my space.
- (Name person) can't impact my energy.
- I will not allow anyone to influence me.
- I am protected against other people's bad intentions.
- I always find my power and will not let anyone take it from me.

- I release all the energies not belonging to me.
- My energy is mine; no one can alter it or take it from me.
- I send positive vibes to the universe and receive good vibes back.
- I am bringing back my strength.
- I call back the energy taken from me.
- I send back the foreign energies not serving me.
- Divine protection is blessing my psychic abilities.
- My mind is safe from psychic attacks.
- My psychic powers are growing, and I control them.
- My shield is strong, psychic attacks bounce off it, and nothing can penetrate it.
- My energy field is protected with divine light, preventing negative influences from reaching me.
- I am protected by a bubble of light; it doesn't allow negativity to touch me.
- I protect my mind from psychic attacks.
- The universe is powerful and protects me against psychic attacks.
- Divine protection protects my body, mind, and spirit from negative influences.
- My guardian angel protects my body and soul.
- My guardian angel is by my side, shielding me from psychic attacks.
- Darkness cannot penetrate my protective shield.
- My guardian angel is keeping me safe.
- I embrace the protection of my spirit guides.

Affirmations to Protect Your Children, Pets, and Loved Ones
- My children are my only priority, and I will keep them safe.
- I place a force field around my family; nothing can penetrate it.
- My pets are surrounded by a powerful protective shield.
- My family, children, pets, and I are loved and safe.

- I surround my family with love and will not allow anyone to hurt them.
- My family and I are strong together, and we are each other's protective shields.
- My family is safe from psychic attacks.
- No one can hurt or influence my loved ones.
- My children and pets are always safe.
- A protective white light surrounds my children and keeps them safe.
- My loved ones are safe from (name person) harm.
- My loved ones are surrounded by a protective shield.
- A shield of light and love keeps my loved ones safe.

Salt Baths for Your Loved Ones

Protect your children and family members from psychic attacks by constantly encouraging them to take salt baths.

Ingredients:
- Salt
- Lavender
- Baking soda

Instructions:
1. Clean your bathtub thoroughly and declutter the bathroom creating a relaxing ambiance.
2. Add a few of their favorite items. If this bath is for your child, add their favorite toy.
3. You can add scented candles, protective crystals, plants, or diffuse essential oils; choose your favorite scents.
4. Play relaxing music.
5. Fill the bathtub with warm water, then add the salt, lavender, and baking soda.
6. Encourage them to take a bath for 20 to 30 minutes.

Protecting Someone from a Distance

You don't have to be in the same room with your children, pet, or family to shield them; you can protect them against psychic attacks from a distance.

Visualization Instructions:
1. Sit on a comfortable chair, close your eyes, and deeply breathe until you feel calm and relaxed.
2. Visualize your loved one surrounded by white protective light.
3. Focus on the image until you see it clearly.
4. Now, think of a happy memory you shared with them. Feel the joy you experienced together on that day, and let the positive vibes flow through you.
5. Spend a couple of minutes contemplating this feeling and your love for them.
6. Imagine these positive emotions have color, and imagine them leaving your body and entering the other person's protective shield.
7. Repeat, *"My loved one is protected by a powerful shield that only allows loving energy in."*

General Tips

- Be mindful of your energy so you can know when you are under psychic attacks.
- Focus on being emotionally stable and strong, so you won't be vulnerable to other people's negativity.
- Never hesitate to seek your guardian angel's or spiritual guide's help to protect you against psychic attacks.
- Whenever you think of the attacker, visualize showering them with pure white light while keeping your protective shield around you. No matter how tempting, never send them the same thoughts or energies they sent you. Remember, you are stronger than them, so meet their fear, hatred, jealousy, and anger with compassion, love, and understanding.

It isn't an exaggeration to say you are regularly under psychic attacks. Shield yourself and your loved ones every day to guarantee other people's darkness and negativity won't affect you. Treat the attacker with love and light. Don't stoop to their level or give in to anger or hatred. Although you can't control their actions, you are in control of your own reactions. Be the better person and return these attacks with positive energy, protecting you, and perhaps you can bring light into their dark world.

Incorporate these techniques into your daily routine. Even if you don't have time to meditate daily, memorize a few affirmations and repeat them when you wake up or on your way to work. Write them down on sticky notes and leave them in various places around the house, so your family can repeat them. Keep your thoughts positive and surround yourself and your loved ones with loving energy.

Chapter 10: Warding Rituals to Protect Your Home

Although shielding yourself and your loved ones against psychic attacks is essential, it won't be enough if your home isn't protected. Imagine you have the flu and taking medication but are constantly exposed to sick people. Will you ever recover? The same applies if you are surrounded by negativity; you will eventually catch these vibes. Your environment should be a sanctuary keeping you protected from psychic attacks.

This chapter covers various methods to shield your home, space, and altar from negative influences and entities.

Shielding your home is just as important as shielding yourself and your loved ones.
https://unsplash.com/photos/1ddol8rgUH8?utm_source=unsplash&utm_medium=referral&utm_content=creditShareLink

Warding Ritual

This ritual works for any physical space. It is a powerful technique to provide your home with permanent protection, so you only need to perform this ritual once in your life. Like a security system, it gives you control over what energies can enter your home and what you won't accept.

Ingredients and Tools:

- 4 jars with lids
- 4 metals or crystals associated with the archangel or deity you are summoning. For instance, if you are calling on the Archangel Gabriel, use aquamarine or citrine. If you summon Uriel, use tigers eye or amber.
- 4 crystals associated with your ancestor or spirit animal.
- 4 air crystals like fluorite, clear quartz, yellow topaz, yellow jasper, blue apatite, barite, or tanzanite
- 4 fire crystals like garnet, ruby, red jasper, carnelian, hematite, amber, sunstone, or pyrite.
- 4 water crystals like blue chalcedony, turquoise, chrysocolla, lapis lazuli, amethyst, chrysoprase, or moonstone
- 4 Earth crystals like emerald, green jade, moss agate, peridot, malachite, black obsidian, or black tourmaline
- 3 dried herbs of choice like lavender, rose petals, juniper, white sage, myrrh, frankincense, angelica root, bay, ginger, or cinnamon
- Pictures of your ancestors
- 1 black candle and 1 white candle
- 1 red tealight candle
- A bundle of purifying herbs like lavender, white sage, palo santo, and cedar
- 1 Bowl of purified water with sea salt

Instructions:

1. Declutter, clean, and organize your home, then purify it using a cleansing ritual.

2. Next, cleanse and shield your spirit.
3. Choose a quiet space with no distractions for your ritual, preferably an altar. Cleanse your altar before starting.
4. Place all the items on the altar to begin your ritual.
5. Sit in a comfortable position, close your eyes, and call on your guardian angel or spirit guide.
6. Set your intention. Say:

    "I cleanse and protect my home from negative energies and influences. I ward my home so it becomes a safe haven of health, abundance, and peace. I will only allow love to enter my home."
7. Light the black and white candles with the intention of banishing the negative influences. Leave them to burn out.
8. Light the herb bundle and the tealight candle. Put them on a heat-safe plate or bowl.
9. Open your front door, hold up the plate so the smoke floats outside the house, and say, "I bless and purify this home with fire and air." Then, draw a pentagram in the air using the smudge stick.
10. Visualize the negative energy blowing out of the door like smoke while repeating, "I bless this home with fire and air."
11. Move the burning herbs clockwise to purify the perimeter of your home. Cleanse the stairs, walls, floors, and every corner of the house. Draw a pentagram in the air near all openings like the fireplace, windows, doors, and mirrors.
12. When you have finished, return to the front door and repeat, "This house is protected by fire and air."
13. Take the bowl of salted water to the front door and repeat, "I bless my home with Earth and Water."
14. Dip your index finger in the water and draw a pentagram on the front door and the door's frame.
15. Visualize all the negativity leaving your home and going out of the front door.
16. Cleanse the perimeter of your home by walking around it clockwise, repeating, "I purify this home with Earth and water," and sprinkling water on the floor and every corner of the house.

17. Dip your finger in the water and draw a pentagram in the air over all the house's openings.
18. When you return to the front door, repeat this phrase: "This house is protected by Earth and water."
19. Return to your altar and repeat:

    "I cleanse and protect my home from negative energies and influences. I ward my home so it becomes a safe haven of health, abundance, and peace. I will only allow love to enter my home."
20. Next, open your jars and put one air crystal, one fire crystal, one water crystal, one Earth crystal, 1 teaspoon of dry herbs, one crystal associated with the archangel you are summoning, and one stone associated with your ancestor or spirit animal in each.
21. Hold each ingredient, blow at it gently, tap it three times, and repeat "awake" to awaken its healing powers. Then repeat "(name the ingredient) strengthen the protective ward around my home." before you drop it in the jar.
22. Summon an archangel associated with the crystal before you put it in the jar, and tell him you seek his protective powers and make an offering in exchange for his help.
23. Write your ancestors' names on a piece of paper and place it near one of the jars with their photos.
24. Ask for their protection and ask them to keep your home safe.
25. You can make an offering to your ancestors, like their favorite drink, food, or flowers, to appease them.
26. Summon your ancestors the same way you summoned the archangel.
27. After placing all the ingredients in the jars, seal them tightly.
28. Hold each jar and repeat:

    "This is a protective ward. May it guard the north side of my home and make it a safe haven of health, abundance, and peace. I will only allow love to enter my home."
29. Repeat the previous step with each jar and say the same intention mentioning a different direction each time (east, west, and south).
30. Tap on each jar with your index finger clockwise and repeat, "Safety, health, abundance, and peace."

31. Visualize an energy cone on top of each jar, feeding and nourishing it to protect your home.
32. Place one jar at the north corner of the house and the other three in the east, west, and south while visualizing threads coming out of each jar, making a big circle encompassing the whole house. (You can place the jars behind the furniture or bury them outdoors.)
33. Return to the altar, express your gratitude, and release all the energies and beings you summoned.

Herbs and Salt

Ingredients:
- 1 cup of sea salt
- ¼ cup of rosemary, raspberry, cinnamon, bay, pepper, and clove

Instructions:
1. Mix the ingredients together in a small bowl.
2. Place the bowl on your altar or at the door of the room you want to protect.

Salt Ritual

Ingredients and Tools:
- Pink Himalayan salt
- Dried bay leaves
- Dried rosemary
- Dried dill
- Cauldron or fire-proof bowl
- Pen and paper

Instructions:
1. Write the word "Protect" on a piece of paper and put it in the fire-proof bowl or cauldron.
2. Cover the piece of paper with the salt and dried herbs.
3. Place your hand over the bowl and visualize negative energy leaving your home and a large white circle enveloping it,

shielding it from psychic attacks.
4. Next, burn the paper, salt, and herbs.
5. After they are burned down, wait for them to cool, then grind them into smaller pieces.
6. Put them in a glass jar, and place the jar anywhere in your home.

This ritual will keep your home safe for a whole year, so you can practice it once a year to protect your home from negative influences.

Practice Yoga

Yoga has always been an effective weapon against negativity since it reduces depression, stress, and anxiety. It has the same effect on physical spaces. Practice yoga in different spaces around the house, like near your altar or in a room you want to protect with the intention of shielding it from negative energy.

Full Moon Protection Ritual

The full moon symbolizes growth and protection. Protective rituals during this time are extremely powerful since lunar energy is a strong weapon against negativity.

Instructions:
1. During a full moon, find a quiet spot in your backyard, garden, or a room indoors with a window open so you can see the moon.
2. Cleanse the space using the white sage smudging ritual.
3. Next, sit comfortably, close your eyes, and take a few deep breaths.
4. Set an intention to protect your home against dark entities.
5. Meditate briefly and feel the moon's energy washing over you and your home.
6. Clear your thoughts and feel your body and mind relaxing.
7. Open your eyes and write on a piece of paper what you want to protect your home against. Repeat it out loud,
8. Hold a clear quartz crystal in your hand and close your eyes
9. Visualize the negativity leaving out the front door and the moon casting a huge protective bubble around your home.

10. Stay with this image for a few minutes. End the session by expressing your gratitude.

Herbs Ritual

Ingredients:

- Dried herbs like pepper, blueberry thrones, burdock root, bay leaves, basil leaves, cloves, and cinnamon.

Instructions:

1. Add all or some of the herbs into a small white pouch bag.
2. Set an intention with every herb, *"This herb will bless my home and shield it from psychic attacks."*
3. Tie the pouch bag with a black or red thread and repeat your intention.
4. Hang the bag on your front door.

Candle Ritual

You can use jar candles, tealight candles, or regular candles. However, jar candles are the best option.

Tools:

- 1 jar candle
- Dried herbs like lavender, basil, bay leaf, cinnamon, rosemary, and sage
- Marker

Instructions:

1. Cleanse the candle using a smudging ritual.
2. Write the word "Protect" on the candle's jar.
3. Light the candle and leave it for a few minutes.
4. Next, sprinkle the herbs over the candle while setting an intention like, *"I intend for these herbs to protect my home from negative influences."*
5. Leave the candle to burn for an hour, then blow it out.
6. Light it every day or every few days to keep your home safe.

Symbols Ritual

Instructions:
1. Draw a protective symbol like the eye of Horus, Hamsa Hand, mistletoe, pentacle, or another symbol on a candle's jar.
2. Light the candle and sit in front of it, staring at the flame.
3. Visualize a protective circle coming out of the flame surrounding your home and shielding it from psychic attacks.

Runes Rituals

Runes are the alphabet in Norse mythology. It comprises twenty-four letters, and all have divine powers.

Tools:
- Flat stone
- Illustrations of protective runes like Algiz, Tiwaz, Ehwaz, Eihwaz, Ingwaz, and Thurisaz

Instructions:
1. Sit in a quiet room and take a few minutes to clear your head.
2. Carve the runes on the flat stone while remaining focused and present in the moment.
3. Set an intention for these runes to fulfill their purpose and protect your home.
4. When you're finished carving, run your hands over the runes while thinking of protecting your home.
5. Choose the rune you feel is powerful enough to shield your home and defend it against psychic attacks. Follow your gut since the right rune will call you.
6. Once you find it, study its shape.
7. Sit comfortably, close your eyes, and take a few deep breaths.
8. Visualize the rune casting a white protective light around your home.
9. Sit with this image for a while.
10. You can also carve the rune on coins and hang them on your front door or elsewhere around the house.

Trataka Meditation

Trataka is an ancient meditation technique usually practiced during a yoga session. It involves intense gazing, focus, and being present in the moment.

Instructions:
1. Place a candle on the floor and light it.
2. Sit in a comfortable position opposite the candle.
3. Gaze at it for three minutes without blinking; you can set a timer beforehand.
4. Expect your eyes to tear up.
5. After three minutes, close your eyes, and the image of the candle's flame will appear to you.
6. Sit with this image for a while until it goes away.
7. Open your eyes and stare at the void between any two objects in the room.
8. This void represents the negativity inside your home.
9. Close your eyes and visualize this void shrinking and disappearing for good.

Crystals Ritual

Tools: Four black tourmaline (or any black crystals

Instructions:
1. You should practice grounding meditation first for this ritual to work.
2. Sit in a comfortable position and close your eyes.
3. Inhale and exhale deeply, focusing on your breath and your chest's movement.
4. Visualize a white light from above entering your body through your ground chakra.
5. Imagine the light moving down your spine, leaving through your feet, and disappearing into the Earth.
6. Feel the negativity inside your body moving down your spine, exiting through your feet, and disappearing into the Earth.

7. Next, visualize pure white light from the Earth entering your body through your feet.
8. Feel the Earth's protection washing over you and repeat, *"I connect with Mother Earth, and she covers me with her protection."*
9. End this session by expressing gratitude to Mother Earth, then open your eyes.
10. You are now ready to practice the crystals ritual.
11. Hold the four black crystals and raise them to the area between your eyebrows (your third eye chakra).
12. Set your intention whether you want to protect your home, specific room, or your altar. Say, *"I program this crystal to protect my space from negative energy."*
13. Place each of the crystals in a different corner around the house. Ensure you place one at the front door to shield your home from negative influences.

Onion Braid

Ingredients:

- Onions with green tops
- 4 feet of twine

Instructions:

1. Fold the twine in half, then tie a knot at its end to create a loop.
2. Put the twine on a flat surface and place an onion upside down. The green tops should form a third string next to the twine's two free ends.
3. Make a tight braid with the three strings.
4. Next, braid the rest of the onions with the twine, focusing on your intention. Say, *"I am making this charm to protect my home and keep negative energy at bay."*
5. Hang them on your front door or on the wall of the room you want to protect.

Charm Ritual

Ingredients:

- Rosemary or yarrow
- 1 protective crystal like malachite, black tourmaline, or smoky quartz
- 1 protective symbol, like crossed spears or Hamsa Hand
- A small bag, preferably black

Instructions:

1. Practice grounding meditation before you perform this ritual.
2. Next, place each item in the bag while visualizing a protective white light emitting from them, creating a protective bubble surrounding your home. The bubble only allows positive and loving energies in and keeps the darkness and negativity at bay.
3. After you put all the items in the bag, place your hand on it. Repeat the Kundalini protection mantra:

    Aad Guray Nameh, "*I call upon the primal wisdom, I bow to the truth that has existed for ages, I summon the true wisdom, I bow to the Divine wisdom.*"
4. Keep repeating the mantra until you sense the energy shifting.
5. Place the bag in the room you want to protect.

Pray to the Four Elements

Instructions:

1. Sit in a comfortable position and take a few deep breaths.
2. Once you feel centered and calm, repeat this chant three times:

    "*Elements of the day and elements of the sun, I beseech you to come my way. I summon the powers of the day and night, and I pray you protect my home.*"
3. Close your eyes and visualize a golden ball of energy surrounding your home, growing bigger and stronger each time you chant.

Affirmations

- My home is protected and guarded.
- My home keeps me safe and secure.

- No unwanted energy can get into my home.
- Only love and light can enter my home.
- The universe places a shield around my home.
- Positive vibrations surround my space.
- My home is protecting me.
- The universe prevents negativity from entering my home.
- I am releasing all unwanted energy from my home.
- Positivity and love emit from my home.
- I prevent negative energy from entering my space.
- The universe is making my home a safe haven.
- No negativity is allowed in my home.
- A strong protective field envelops my home; nothing can get in.
- All negative influences are released from my home.
- There is no room in my space for fear and anxiety.
- Only positive vibes are welcomed in my home.
- My space emits positivity and peace.
- My space is protected from bad vibes.
- My home protects my energy.
- My loved ones are safe in my home.
- I am grateful for the positive energy shielding my space.
- Divine protection keeps my home safe.
- My home is a magnet, only attracting love and positivity.
- I am protected from negative influences.
- I am grateful for the divine's protection.
- I choose to feel safe in my space.
- Bad energy can't penetrate my home's shield.
- I am safe in my surroundings.
- Nothing bad can happen. My space keeps me safe.
- I welcome the universe's protection.
- My home vibrates positive energy.

- I am not afraid. I feel secure in my environment.
- I am cleansing my space of negative influences.
- My home is my boundary; it keeps me safe.
- I release the negativity from my home to free space for love and abundance.
- Nothing can get into my house without my permission.
- My home only welcomes positive energy.
- Protective energy guards my space.
- Positivity and wisdom surround my space.
- My home is free of negative energies.
- My guardian angel is watching over my space.

Negative influences can easily find their way into your home. Practice any of these rituals whenever you feel a shift in energy or bad vibes is taking over your space. Always protect your home by placing protective symbols, crystals, herbs, or an onion braid around your home.

Conclusion

You've reached the end of this book and are significantly more informed about your psychic energy and those around you, particularly negative energies and attacks. Even when you're confident of being in a positive space and energy, negativity can attack, *but now you know how to deal with it.*

Psychic attacks can significantly impact your mood and mental and physical health. They can lower your home's vibration and spread negativity to every aspect of your life. Avoiding negative energy isn't realistic since people and objects carry bad vibes influencing you daily. However, practicing certain cleansing rituals and spiritual work can shield you from negativity and low vibrations.

The book began by explaining the concept of psychic attacks and negative energy. It provided exercises so you could better understand how energy works, and then we discussed psychic protection and its many benefits.

You can't protect yourself against psychic attacks without raising your vibration and sharpening your psychic skills first. The second chapter provided multiple instructions and tips, including breathing exercises, meditation, and visualization techniques to prepare your psyche for protection. Your soul and karma also require cleansing to clear past energies and influences so you are ready to receive positive energy. The book included effective techniques to purify your soul and discussed the concept of karma, how external influences alter it, and what you can do to protect yourself.

Negative energy can impact your home, pets, and family. The book discussed how to identify negative energy in your home and provided multiple cleansing rituals you can perform to cleanse your space and loved ones.

The word "aura" is often mentioned during discussions of the psyche and spiritual work. The book explains this concept in detail and its connection to the soul. Negative energy is powerful enough to damage your aura. The book discussed identifying when it is damaged and various healing techniques. It explained the significance of a strong aura against psychic attacks.

Every person has a guardian angel helping, protecting, and guiding them. The book explains the role of these angels in your life and how you can summon them to defend yourself or a loved one against psychic attacks.

After providing all the information to prepare yourself for protection, the book's second part focuses on self-defense against psychic attacks, introducing symbols, plants, crystals, and their protective purposes. Then, it focused on curses, hexes, and unwanted attachments by defining each concept and how to recognize if you are a victim. It covered multiple rituals and methods to break these spells.

You are constantly exposed to psychic attacks wherever you go, but if you can protect yourself against these influences, you can keep yourself and your loved ones safe. The last part of the book focused on protection techniques to use on yourself, your family, and your pets. It provided warding rituals to protect your home, space, and altar.

Let this book guide you and use all the rituals, tips, and techniques mentioned to shield yourself and everything you hold dear from psychic attacks.

Here's another book by Mari Silva that you might like

Your Free Gift
(only available for a limited time)

Thanks for getting this book! If you want to learn more about various spirituality topics, then join Mari Silva's community and get a free guided meditation MP3 for awakening your third eye. This guided meditation mp3 is designed to open and strengthen ones third eye so you can experience a higher state of consciousness. Simply visit the link below the image to get started.

https://spiritualityspot.com/meditation

References

The College of Psychic Studies : Enlighten : What is a psychic attack. (n.d.). The College of Psychic Studies. https://www.collegeofpsychicstudies.co.uk/enlighten/what-is-a-psychic-attack/

Leigh, J. (2018, May 31). Psychic Protection. Spirituality & Health. https://www.spiritualityhealth.com/articles/2018/05/31/psychic-protection

Mara. (2011, July 22). Boundaries and Psychic Protection. WholeSpirit → Shamanic Counselor ∴ Intuitive Consultant ∴ Energy Healer ∴ Personal Evolution Through Nature-Based Shamanic Healing & Shamanic Training. https://www.wholespirit.com/boundaries-and-psychic-protection/

Boundaries and psychic protection ∴ WholeSpirit. (2011, July 22). WholeSpirit → Shamanic Counselor ∴ Intuitive Consultant ∴ Energy Healer ∴ Personal Evolution Through Nature-Based Shamanic Healing & Shamanic Training; Whole Spirit LLC. https://www.wholespirit.com/boundaries-and-psychic-protection/

Earthmonk. (2022, January 7). 8 powerful ways to protect your spiritual energy. Earthmonk. https://earthmonk.guru/8-powerful-ways-to-protect-spiritual-energy/

Insight Network, Inc. (n.d.). Insight timer - #1 free meditation app for sleep, relax & more. Insighttimer.com. https://insighttimer.com/stevenobel/guided-meditations/psychic-protection-meditation

Leigh, J. (2018, May 31). Psychic protection. Spirituality & Health. https://www.spiritualityhealth.com/articles/2018/05/31/psychic-protection

Stardust, L. (2019, May 28). How to use magic to banish energy vampires. Teen Vogue. https://www.teenvogue.com/story/how-to-use-magic-to-banish-energy-vampires

Why protection is important in healing and psychic work. (2022, March 10). Giancarlo Serra. https://www.giancarloserra.org/why-protection-is-important-in-healing-and-psychic-work/

Zukav, G. (2015, April 1). How to protect your spiritual energy. Oprah.com. https://www.oprah.com/inspiration/protecting-your-spiritual-energy

Cass. (2022, August 7). 5 meditations to raise your vibration. Manifesting Harmony. https://manifestingharmony.com/tools/meditations-to-raise-your-vibration/

Coughlin, S. (2015, October 21). 5 medium-approved tips to develop your own psychic powers. Refinery29.com; Refinery29. https://www.refinery29.com/en-us/how-to-improve-intuition

Cronkleton, E. (2018, May 15). What is aromatherapy and how does it help me? Healthline. https://www.healthline.com/health/what-is-aromatherapy

Estrada, J. (2019, September 11). What it actually means to raise your vibrational energy—plus 12 ways to do it. Well+Good. https://www.wellandgood.com/vibrational-energy/

How to raise your vibration instantly? (2021, May 21). Times of India Blog. https://timesofindia.indiatimes.com/readersblog/theenchantedpen/how-to-raise-your-vibration-instantly-32251/

Irven, J. (2020, March 29). 19 ways to raise your vibration — sustainable bliss. Sustainable Bliss | Self-Care and Intentional Living. https://www.sustainableblissco.com/journal/raising-your-vibration

Jones, E. (2009). Aromatherapy. In Massage for Therapists (pp. 163–178). Wiley-Blackwell.

Mahakatha, A. (2023, January 16). Best guided meditation to raise vibration. Mahakatha Blog. https://mahakatha.com/blog/best-guided-meditation-to-raise-vibration

McGinley, K. (2019, September 18). How to raise your emotional & spiritual vibration. Chopra. https://chopra.com/articles/a-complete-guide-to-raise-your-vibration

Raypole, C. (2021, May 5). Metta meditation for mother's day.

Rebecca Joy Stanborough, M. F. A. (2020, November 13). What is vibrational energy? Healthline. https://www.healthline.com/health/vibrational-energy

Rose, S. (2022, February 28). 15 ways to raise your vibrations. Sahara Rose. https://iamsahararose.com/blog/a-guide-on-how-to-raise-your-vibrations/

Sara. (2021, April 10). 35 affirmations to raise your vibration instantly. Spiritvibez. https://spiritvibez.com/35-affirmations-to-raise-your-vibration/

Top 4 breathing practices to raise your vibration. (2020, May 20). YogaVibes. https://www.yogavibes.com/blog/meditation-pranayama/raise-vibration-breathing-practice/

What is reiki, and does it really work? (2021, August 30). Cleveland Clinic. https://health.clevelandclinic.org/reiki/

Basic Buddhist teachings - III. (2021, April 14). Theravada. https://www.theravada.gr/en/about-buddhism/understanding-karma/

Darren. (2012, March 7). The 4 dimensions of energy: Physical, emotional, mental and spiritual. UpStartist. https://upstartist.tv/mba/the-4-dimensions-of-energy/

Stuck feeling stagnant? 14 spiritual cleansing methods to clear it out. (2023, February 24). Mindbodygreen. https://www.mindbodygreen.com/articles/spiritual-cleansing

Thomas, P. (2019, October 9). Your 4 types of energy. Self Help for Life. https://selfhelpforlife.com/master-your-energy/

(N.d.-a). Yogabasics.comhttps://www.yogabasics.com/connect/yoga-blog/spiritual-cleansing/

(N.d.-b). Goop.comhttps://goop.com/wellness/spirituality/the-four-bodies/

6 ways to purify your space – KonMari. (2019, November 12). KonMari | The Official Website of Marie Kondo; KonMari Media, Inc. https://konmari.com/home-purification/

10 easy ways to cleanse your home of negative energy. (2012, April 3). Mindbodygreen. https://www.mindbodygreen.com/articles/how-to-cleanse-your-home-of-negative-energy

Bunch, E. (2019, April 3). 4 ways to set the right intention for your home with a cleansing prayer. Well+Good. https://www.wellandgood.com/prayer-to-say-when-saging-your-house/

Davis, F. (2022, April 11). Spiritual pet protection: Shield your dog or cat in positive energy. Karma and Luck. https://www.karmaandluck.com/blogs/news/spiritual-pet-protection

Helena. (2021, January 24). How to build an altar at home for spiritual self-care. Disorient.

How to clear negative energy around baby or older children. (n.d.). Go with Harmony. https://www.gowithharmony.com/clear-negative-energy-around-baby.html

Jay, S. (2022, August 3). 6 cleansing rituals for you & your home. Revoloon. https://revoloon.com/shanijay/cleansing-ritual

Oaks, M. (2020, September 29). House cleansing: A checklist for clearing bad energy from your home. Redfin | Real Estate Tips for Home Buying, Selling & More; Redfin. https://www.redfin.com/blog/clearing-bad-energy-from-your-home/

PURNAMA. (2020, July 15). Jak okadzać dom by pozbyć się negatywnej energii? PURNAMA.

Sanna. (2021, April 27). How to Cleanse the Energy in your Space using Incense. SANNA Conscious Concept. https://sannaconsciousconcept.com/how-to-cleanse-the-energy-in-your-space-using-incense

Stewart, T. (2021, October 17). Step by step: How to cleanse A space (energetically & spiritually). Whimsy Soul. https://whimsysoul.com/how-to-cleanse-a-space-energetically-and-spiritually/

The importance of purifying and cleansing your space before a big move. (2021, February 23).

Tiny carbons cure to clear negative energy you absorbed from other people. (n.d.). Go with Harmony. https://www.gowithharmony.com/cure-to-clear-negative-energy.html

Tuttle, C. (2020, October 19). 2 techniques to protect your child from negative energy. Carol Tuttle. https://ct.liveyourtruth.com/2-techniques-to-protect-your-child-from-negative-energy/

Why energy cleansing is important (and how to do it). (n.d.). AUTHOR KAREN FRAZIER. https://www.authorkarenfrazier.com/blog/why-energy-cleansing-is-important-and-how-to-do-it#/

(N.d.). Yogabasics.com. https://www.yogabasics.com/connect/yoga-blog/clear-negative-energy/

7 ways to reset your energy & cleanse your aura when you feel blocked. (2022, September 21). Mindbodygreen. https://www.mindbodygreen.com/articles/aura-cleansing

Marley, C. (2018, November 25). How to cleanse aura. Mental Health Resources & Articles | Plumm; Plummhealth. https://blog.plummhealth.com/fundamental-concepts/8-ways-to-cleanse-your-aura-from-negativity/

Tanaaz. (2016, April 26). The 7 layers of your aura. Forever Conscious. https://foreverconscious.com/7-layers-aura

Who stole my energy? How difficult people affect your aura. (2012, July 26). Mindbodygreen. https://www.mindbodygreen.com/articles/how-difficult-people-affect-your-aura-energy

(N.d.). Goop.com. https://goop.com/wellness/spirituality/healing-your-aura/

Bernstein, G. (2019, December 22). A Spirit Junkie Introduction to Archangels and Guardian Angels. Gabby Bernstein. https://gabbybernstein.com/angels/

pakosloski. (2022, April 6). Guardian Angel prayer for spiritual protection. Aleteia — Catholic Spirituality, Lifestyle, World News, and Culture. https://aleteia.org/2022/04/06/guardian-angel-prayer-for-spiritual-protection/

Insight Network, Inc. (n.d.). Psychic Protection With Archangel Michael. Insighttimer.Com. https://insighttimer.com/sarahhall444/guided-meditations/psychic-protection-with-archangel-michael

Richardson, T. C. (2021, May 25). How To Get To Know Your Guardian Angels + Unlock Their Power. Mindbodygreen. https://www.mindbodygreen.com/articles/how-to-get-to-know-your-guardian-angels

Megan, M. (2020, October 5). Divine Angel Summoning Sigils - Magick Megan. Medium. https://medium.com/@matohinlef7/divine-angel-summoning-sigils-b75c2d70b620

eskarda. (2021, August 18). 5 Crystals for Protection From Negative Energy. Yoga Journal. https://www.yogajournal.com/lifestyle/crystals-for-protection/

Skon, J. (2023, January 13). 6 Crystals To Protect Yourself From Toxic People & Negative Energy. Mindbodygreen. https://www.mindbodygreen.com/articles/crystals-for-protection

Top 15 Spiritual Plants. (2020, December 24). Floweraura Blog. https://www.floweraura.com/blog/plants-care-n-tips/top-10-spiritual-plants

Growing, B. (2021, August 31). How To Use Houseplants for Spiritual Protection (14 Plants). Bean Growing. https://www.beangrowing.com/houseplants-for-spiritual-protection/

Vierck, J. (2022, March 23). Top 8 Powerful Protection Symbols & How to Use Them. Karma and Luck. https://www.karmaandluck.com/blogs/news/8-powerful-protection-symbols-how-to-use-them

Wang, C. (2022, May 10). 7 Spiritual Protection Symbols and Their Meanings. Buddha & Karma. https://buddhaandkarma.com/blogs/guide/spiritual-protection-symbols-meaning

Jennifer McVey, C. (2022, June 14). How to Make Sigils. WikiHow. https://www.wikihow.com/Make-Sigils

Kallima Spiritual Centre - Newsletter - July/August 2020. (n.d.). Flipbuilder.Com. https://online.flipbuilder.com/yjll/isyd/files/basic-html/page15.html

Wood, T. (2021, October 21). 10 Signs of Spiritual Attack. Evergreen Church. https://evcsj.org/2021-10-21-10-signs-of-spiritual-attack/

6 Easy Ways To Break A Magic Curse Or Hex. (2022, March 5). Eclectic Witchcraft. https://eclecticwitchcraft.com/break-a-magic-curse-or-hex/

Rose, M. (2022, December 8). StyleCaster. StyleCaster. https://stylecaster.com/how-to-use-protection-magic/

Alex. (2021, October 1). 83+ positive affirmations for spiritual protection (psychic energy). Manifest Like Whoa! https://manifestlikewhoa.com/positive-affirmations-spiritual-protection/

Avantika. (2020, December 23). 9 proven ways to protect yourself from psychic Attacks. BigBrainCoach. https://bigbraincoach.com/psychic-attacks/

Five ways to protect yourself from psychic attacks. (n.d.). Gaia https://www.gaia.com/article/protect-yourself-from-psychic-attacks

How to Create A Personal Energy Shield for Protection - abundance coach for women in business. (2022, February 23). Abundance Coach for Women in Business | Evelyn Lim. https://www.evelynlim.com/how-to-create-a-personal-energy-shield-for-protection/

How to smudge or hold a space clearing ceremony in your home. (2019, October 23). Glad.Is. https://glad.is/blogs/articles/how-smudge-or-hold-a-space-clearing-ceremony-in-your-home

Milazzo, N. (2022). Binaural Beats Research Analysis. https://examine.com/other/binauralbeats/

Original Products. (2021, May 18). Spiritual protection against psychic attacks. Original Botanica; www.originalbotanica.com#creator. https://originalbotanica.com/blog/spiritual-protection-against-psychic-attacks

Pawula, S. (2011, September 17). How to create a self-protective bubble —. Always Well Within. https://www.alwayswellwithin.com/blog/2011/09/18/vulnerability-and-protection

Peterson, K. (2020, September 5). Spiritual bath: DIY energy cleanse. Balance. https://www.balance-withus.com/blog/spiritual-bath-diy-energy-cleanse/

Sangimino, M. (2020, July 20). Meditation script: Protecting your energy. Soul & Sea. https://medium.com/soul-sea/meditation-script-protecting-your-energy-243d7929af3d

Tanaaz. (2015, March 11). 9 ways to protect yourself from psychic attacks. Forever Conscious. https://foreverconscious.com/9-ways-to-protect-yourself-from-psychic-attacks

The College of Psychic Studies : Enlighten : What is a psychic attack. (n.d.). The College of Psychic Studies. https://www.collegeofpsychicstudies.co.uk/enlighten/what-is-a-psychic-attack/

6 crystals to protect yourself from toxic people & negative energy. (2020, February 11). Mindbodygreen. https://www.mindbodygreen.com/articles/crystals-for-protection

9 powerful Air element crystals for inspiration. (2021, November 15). Crystals Alchemy. https://crystalsalchemy.com/air-element-crystals

9 powerful Earth element crystals for abundance. (2021, November 15). Crystals Alchemy. https://crystalsalchemy.com/earth-element-crystals

9 powerful Water element crystals for love and inner peace. (2021, November 17). Crystals Alchemy. https://crystalsalchemy.com/water-element-crystals

Darcy. (2022, August 4). Rune for protection – your guide for the meanings and use of Norse runes. Mythology Merchant. https://www.mythologymerchant.com/rune-for-protection-your-guide-for-the-meanings-and-use-of-norse-runes/

De Leonardis, K. (2022, May 3). 6 ways to energetically cleanse & protect your home – Lynn Hazan. Lynnhazan.com. https://lynnhazan.com/lifestyle/6-ways-to-energetically-cleanse-protect-your-home/

Fire Element Crystals: 9 best healing stones to balance your elements. (2021, November 14). Crystals Alchemy. https://crystalsalchemy.com/fire-element-crystals

Greenwood, C. (2021, December 10). 9 protection rituals to protect your space and energy. Outofstress.com. https://www.outofstress.com/protection-rituals/

Infusing folk magic into your home (with magical protection salt). (n.d.). Beccapiastrelli.com. https://beccapiastrelli.com/house-witchery/

Insight Network, Inc. (n.d.). Insight timer - #1 free meditation app for sleep, relax & more. Insighttimer.com. https://insighttimer.com/kathrynmccusker/guided-meditations/kundalini-mantra-meditation-aad-guray-nameh-protection

Johnson, E. (n.d.). 3 simple protection rituals. Zennedout.com. https://zennedout.com/3-simple-protection-rituals/

Kristenson, S. (2022, May 6). 60 protection affirmations to feel safe & secure. Happier Human; Steve Scott. https://www.happierhuman.com/protection-affirmations/

Michelle, H. (2017, August 12). Warding Ritual for Spiritual Protection of your Home. Witch on Fire. https://www.patheos.com/blogs/witchonfire/2017/08/warding-ritual-protection/

Rose, M. (2022, December 8). How to use protection magic: 5 spells that clear negative energy. StyleCaster. https://stylecaster.com/how-to-use-protection-magic/

Thorp, T. (2019, February 4). Guided meditation: Ground yourself using the Earth element. Chopra. https://chopra.com/articles/guided-meditation-ground-yourself-using-the-earth-element

Tim, & Marieke. (2020, February 1). Aad Guray Nameh - mantra for protection. Kundalini Yoga School. https://kundaliniyogaschool.org/2020/02/01/aad-guray-nameh-mantra-protection-kundalini-yoga/

Vialet B Rayne, C. (1566601033000). Archangels and their crystals. Linkedin.com. https://www.linkedin.com/pulse/archangels-crystals-vialet-b-rayne-crmt/

Wigington, P. (2009, July 5). Protection Magic. Learn Religions. https://www.learnreligions.com/magic-protection-spells-and-rituals-2562176

Minotra, T. (2022, July 5). 70+ powerful Affirmations for Protection & safety. ThediaryforLife. https://www.thediaryforlife.com/affirmations-for-protection-safety

Printed in Dunstable, United Kingdom